BRIGHTON'S
SECRET AGENTS

UNIFORM

This edition first published in 2016 by Uniform
an imprint of Unicorn Publishing Group LLP

101 Wardour Street
London
W1F 0UG
www.unicornpublishing.org

ISBN 978-1-910500-75-0

Printed in Great Britain

BRIGHTON'S SECRET AGENTS

THE BRIGHTON & HOVE CONTRIBUTION TO
BRITAIN'S WW2 SPECIAL OPERATIONS EXECUTIVE (SOE)

PAUL McCUE

UNIFORM

CONTENTS

INTRODUCTION

THE GENESIS OF THIS BOOK CAME FROM A PROJECT FOR FOUR BLUE plaques to commemorate four Brighton-born officers of Britain's Special Operations Executive (SOE) during the Second World War. The blue plaques are an initiative of the Secret WW2 Learning Network, an educational charity founded by Martyn Bell and Martyn Cox, both also Brighton-born.

As a Trustee of the charity, my involvement began when it came to our attention that there were three agents of French Section SOE who served in occupied France and who had been born in Brighton, a fact that naturally aroused the interest of the two Martyns and led to the proposal to honour the agents with blue plaques in Brighton and Hove. As planning progressed, Ryan Gearing of Unicorn Press became interested and involved, discovered a fourth SOE officer who had served in Italy, and suggested a book on the four subjects.

Due to my already being an SOE historian and author, the task fell to me and thanks to my existing research I have been able to add additional elements in respect of five others who had links to the Brighton area (largely in terms of education in Brighton and Hove) and who either served in, or supported, SOE. This book is the end result and chiefly aims to provide the background to the service of the four blue plaque recipients – Lieutenant Jacqueline Nearne, Captain Ron Taylor, Captain Michael Trotobas and Captain Edward Zeff.

My thanks go to those many people who have helped me. I have added relevant acknowledgements (and sources) after each case study, but special mention must be made of the text processing assistance that I have had from Sue Spencer, with additional support from Louisa Russell, and of Jo Bewley for proof reading.

All profit from sales of the book will go to the charity, to enable the Secret WW2 Learning Network to continue bringing little-known exploits such as those of these four officers, to the wider public and future generations.

Paul McCue
November 2016

NOTES TO THE TEXT

IN LINE WITH THE FORMAT ADOPTED BY THE LATE PROFESSOR MICHAEL Foot for the official history '*SOE in France*', codenames are given in capital letters, e.g. DESIGNER, and field names in italics, e.g. *Jacqueline*.

The various German police and intelligence agencies operating in France during the Second World War were numerous (e.g. the *Sicherheitsdienst*, the *Abwehr*, the *Geheime feldpolizei*, the *Gestapo*), but unless specified otherwise, I have used the generic term Gestapo, as indeed did SOE and the *Résistance* during the war. In reality, the *Sicherheitsdienst* of the SS and the German military intelligence service, the *Abwehr*, were very active against SOE, with some notable successes.

To help identify the location of French towns, the *département* code is put in brackets after the town's name e.g. Tarbes (65).

I trust that my French friends will forgive the anglicised spelling of locations such as Lyons and Marseilles.

PART 1

THE SPECIAL OPERATIONS EXECUTIVE (SOE)

Chapter 1

THE BIRTH OF SOE

THE SPECIAL OPERATIONS EXECUTIVE WAS A BRITISH SECRET SERVICE founded in 1940. Its creation was due to the common, if erroneous, belief that the victories achieved by the Germans up to that summer had been won not just by military might, but also by strong fifth columnist elements within the countries that had fallen. Though this belief was largely, indeed almost entirely, wrong, it nevertheless encouraged the British to further investigate subversive warfare and to create a new service to deliver it.

Prime Minister Winston Churchill (above left) is widely-credited with being responsible for founding SOE, but it was Neville Chamberlain (above right), then Lord Chancellor, who drafted the organisation's charter. Photos: author's coll.

As is relatively well-known, it was then Prime Minister Winston Churchill who, fired with enthusiasm for a Special Operations Executive, issued the instruction that would go down in history: 'And now set Europe ablaze'. But the document that effectively laid out SOE's terms of reference and aims was drafted by a very different character to Churchill. Neville Chamberlain, then the Lord President, but previously the Prime Minister before Churchill, was the British leader who had stumbled into the trap of appeasement in 1938 after so drastically misjudging the intentions of Herr Hitler. Though Chamberlain fell ill and died only a few months after his draft first saw the light of day, it was perhaps fitting that one of the last achievements of this much-criticised man was to help lay the foundations of a service which was to operate at the very opposite end of the spectrum from appeasement – by taking the fight to the enemy.

But 1940 was the year when Britain was fighting for its very existence, against a powerful enemy flushed with success. There was therefore no time to be lost in creating this new secret service which reported to (later Sir) Hugh Dalton, the Minister for Economic Warfare. Dalton swiftly recruited Gladwyn Jebb, later Lord Gladwyn, as the organisation's chief executive officer, and Sir Frank Nelson, a former MP, as the first head of the sabotage branch of the new body. Together and individually they quickly and confidentially spread the word to a necessary few people in government and the armed services, explaining what SOE was and how it ought to be supported. It was always made clear that Churchill's personal *imperium* lay behind the new service, whose basic aims were described as: immediate or short-term sabotage; long-term planned sabotage to support allied military requirements; and the recruitment, training and arming of secret armies, ready to rise up in enemy-occupied territories on receipt of instructions from headquarters.

Above (left to right): Hugh Dalton, Gladwyn Jebb and Sir Frank Nelson were early architects of SOE. Photos: author's coll.

Three separate agencies, each possessing some degree of specialist knowledge or ability in the black arts of sabotage, subversion and propaganda, were amalgamated to form

SOE. Of the three: MI R was a little-known military intelligence research branch of the War Office; EH (Electra House) was a highly-secret propaganda section in the Foreign Office; and Section D (D reputedly standing for Destruction) was an equally-inadmissible element within the Secret Intelligence Service (SIS, also known as MI6). SOE was to be so secret that not even Parliament, let alone the British public, was informed of its creation.

SIS, the most senior and established of Britain's secret services, was already charged with work outside the British Isles and was particularly resentful and suspicious of the new upstart service. This rivalry with SOE lasted throughout much of the war, though relations did improve as the conflict progressed. Early distrust was exacerbated, however, when Sir Stewart Menzies, the Director General of SIS, only discovered three weeks after the event that Section D had passed from his control to SOE. Moreover, SIS had good reason for wanting to keep SOE at arm's length. The role of SIS was the gathering of intelligence as quietly and subtly as possible, while SOE's job of creating havoc was almost always certain to provoke a violent enemy response. Menzies continued to take opportunities to undermine the fledgling organisation throughout the war and found allies among some of the senior officers of RAF Bomber Command, who resented having to loan aircraft for SOE's 'unethical' clandestine missions and begrudged any aircraft diverted from their over-riding aim of bombing Germany.

In February 1942, Dalton was replaced as Minister by Roundell Palmer, The Earl of Selborne, a personal friend of Churchill. Three months later Sir Charles Hambro took over as Executive Director (known as 'CD') when Sir Frank Nelson retired through ill-health. Hambro, an old Etonian merchant banker, prominent figure in the City of London, Chairman of the Great Western Railway and late of the Coldstream Guards, had previously served as head of SOE's Scandinavian Section and so was an experienced insider. Below him, Brigadier Colin Gubbins was in command of SOE's western European operations and was to replace Hambro in September 1943 when the latter resigned over a disagreement with Selborne over policy.

Brigadier, later Major-General, later Sir, Colin Gubbins, proved a formidable talent. Prior to joining SOE he had been responsible for creating the Auxiliary Units, the stay-behind forces designed to harry the Germans in the event of a successful invasion of the British Isles. From his former command he brought with him several of his most resourceful and able officers who were to give SOE a remarkable backbone of talented staff. He commenced as SOE's Director of Operations and Training in November 1940, shortly after SOE took up residence in London's Baker Street, close to the headquarters of Marks and Spencer, some of whose requisitioned offices they used. As a career military man, Gubbins was at first viewed with some suspicion, but he soon proved his grasp of, and commitment to, unorthodox methods and this was recognised when he replaced Hambro as CD. In addition to his talent for irregular warfare, Gubbins also seems to have encompassed the art of sidestepping much bureaucracy and administrative requirement. One example of this was that everyone employed by SOE, including those who never left England, paid no income tax on his or her salary.

Above: (left to right), the Earl of Selborne; Sir Charles Hambro and Brigadier Colin Gubbins.
Photos: author's coll.

Chapter 2

OPERATIONS IN FRANCE

AS THREE OF THE BLUE PLAQUE RECIPIENTS, AND THREE OF THE ADDI-
tional five case studies, relate to agents of French Section, SOE the following two chapters
concentrate on the training and despatch on operations of agents destined for France.

After the promotion of Gubbins to the post of CD, Colonel Robin Brook commanded
those sections involved in western Europe, these generally being divided up on a country-
by-country basis. With regard to operations in France, however, the picture was much
more complicated. F (French) Section, which was commanded from 1941 by Major (later
Colonel) Maurice Buckmaster, formerly a manager of the Ford Motor Company in pre-war
Paris, was informally known as the 'independents'. There was then RF (*République Française*)
Section, nominally commanded by a British SOE officer, but reporting to De Gaulle who
consequently treated the 'independents' of F Section with distrust. Both F and RF Sections
operated agents into France from England, but despite their both belonging to SOE, there
was no liaison or joint operations in the field. To muddy the waters further, AMF Section
also dispatched agents from Algiers in north Africa, mainly just to southern France. EU/P,
the Polish SOE section, sent at least 28 agents to work with the sizeable Polish ex-patriot
community in France, but they too kept to themselves. There were also a dozen or so
agents in France from DF, SOE's section that ran several highly-successful escape lines
for shot-down airmen, evading prisoners of war and the like. And finally, from D-Day
onwards, SOE sent 'Jedburghs' to France. Small (normally three-man) inter-allied teams of
advisers, their job was to support and supply the rapidly-expanding resistance forces and to
encourage them in rising up against the enemy.

All this activity took time to develop. SOE's first operation into France did not take place until March 1941, when RF Section parachuted six men into southern Brittany in an unsuccessful attempt to attack the crews of a specialist pathfinder squadron of the *Luftwaffe*. F Section were only slightly behind when they parachuted a radio operator, Georges Bégué, into the Châteauroux (36) area of France in May 1941, followed by his circuit organiser, Philipe de Vomécourt, a few days later. From this somewhat cautious start, a steady stream of agents was sent to France to encourage and arm the various factions of French resistance.

The process for the recruitment of agents often involved a preliminary interview in an anonymous annexe of the War Office, the former Hotel Victoria at 8 Northumberland Avenue in central London, currently a bar, brasserie and event facility. Interviewees would wait in a reception room until called into a dark, bleak and bare room, inadequately lit by one naked light bulb and furnished only with the minimum necessities of a table, two hard kitchen chairs and a blackout curtain. SOE's recruiting officers included characters such as Major Lewis Gielgud, the brother of the famous actor (later Sir) John Gielgud and Captain Selwyn Jepson, a prolific author of murder mysteries and screenplays and credited with being SOE's best 'talent spotter'.

To put the applicant at an initial disadvantage, the interviewing officer would often reveal that he already knew some obscure fact or detail about the interviewee, preferably something that would surprise and unsettle the would-be agent. This might involve a comment on something that the interviewee had done the day before, showing that they had been shadowed. After a few introductory words the interviewer would switch to French, since the applicant's language skills and knowledge of the country had to be assessed. It was also important to make an initial assessment of character and motivation for wanting to be considered for some kind of special duty.

At this stage many candidates still had little or no idea why they were there and some were still anticipating interpreting or translation work. Such notions were soon dispelled when the interviewer posed questions such as: do you want to serve your country better? have you ever flown? how do you feel about parachuting from an aeroplane? and are you courageous enough to be dropped into enemy territory? In fairness to the applicant, the dangers were explicitly described and the warning given that one could expect a slow and painful death if caught. It was stressed that it was a volunteer job and the candidate was given the chance to go away and think about it a little more, before making a decision. It was also made clear that if he or she decided not to carry on, then that decision would be understood and accepted.

Up to three interviews could be held and would be accompanied by security vetting that was carried out by MI5, the British secret Security Service that operated on home soil. This process verified the candidate's loyalty and good character and with this confirmed, a final interview would cover more detail about the work that might be involved. At this point, the recruit began to understand a little more of the extent of SOE's work, though the actual title of 'SOE' was still rarely, if ever, mentioned or used. The cover name for the organisation was the Inter-Services Research Bureau (ISRB), but it was generally referred to only as 'The Racket', 'The Outfit', or 'The Firm' by those who worked for, or who knew of, it. The interviewing officer again stressed the potential dangers, together with the sobering advice that there might only be a 50/50 chance of survival.

The former Hotel Victoria at 8 Northumberland Avenue in London, used by SOE for interviewing potential agents. Photo: author.

Once cleared for training as an agent, the recruit would receive £1 per day while under training, paid from special, rather than from Army, funds. On their service record they would receive the term 'specially employed', the term used to describe, or rather not describe, the work of SOE's agents. Those agents destined for F Section would then report to Norgeby House, a new building that had been destined for the Treasury, but had been requisitioned as F Section's headquarters, ideally located as it was directly across the road from SOE's head office at 64 Baker Street. After administrative formalities at Norgeby House, the recruit would then report to Orchard Court, a tall and imposing block of flats with a roomy entrance hall, thick carpets, and uniformed porters, located a short walk away in Portman Square. There, SOE's F Section used a spacious six-room apartment on the third floor, remembered by many for its black-tiled bathroom, which was often pressed into service for general office use. Also fondly-remembered and a highly-popular figure, was Park, a pre-war messenger for a British bank in Paris who was responsible for reception duties at the flat. It was his job to ensure that agents did not see too much of each other (except where they were in the same team) and he achieved this with considerable diplomacy, helped by an impressive memory for agents' codenames. The Orchard Court apartment had an atmosphere of simplicity and efficiency, with everyone seeming to work long hours and with rank apparently holding little meaning. Despite its distinctly unmilitary appearance, the apartment, together with the Baker Street offices, constituted a vital element of SOE's world-wide network, from Europe to the Middle and Far East, Africa and Canada.

It was at Orchard Court that recruits met their future training classmates. Recruits were of all types, some in uniform, some in civilian clothes and their wide variety of backgrounds bore testimony to SOE's willingness to recruit without prejudice. Taxi drivers and shop assistants rubbed shoulders with barristers and public school masters. There were at least two glamorous former racing drivers, a gay music hall entertainer, and numerous women who at that time were still a novelty in operational roles in Britain's armed wartime services. Among the latter were a Chilean actress and an American woman journalist with a wooden leg. Some of the recruits were motivated by loyalty to England, to France, or to both, some by a personal hatred of the Germans. The one thing they had in common was that they were almost all amateurs at this dangerous and secret work and men and women were offered the rare opportunity to work together as equals because women could pass into occupied territory unnoticed, unlike men of military age.

Above: (left) (SOE's headquarters were at 64 Baker Street in London and French Section used an apartment at nearby Orchard Court in Portman Square (right). Photos: author.

CHAPTER 2 – OPERATIONS IN FRANCE

At Orchard Court the trainees would learn that they were to be sent on a preliminary course, which would commence their training, but more importantly would also give F Section's staff a further opportunity to size up the trainee. If at the end of it the recruit wanted to pack up and go, then that would still be acceptable, though those who decided to drop-out, or were found wanting, were sent off to the north of Scotland. There, at SOE's workshops at Inverlair in Inverness-shire, they would work on low-key duties such as the production of operational equipment for SOE and the creation of an assault course for street fighting, complete with moving dummies and targets, which was a forerunner of the facilities still in use today by police and military forces. Thus usefully engaged, they would be held almost completely incommunicado for several months until whatever knowledge they had gained, particularly of the people they had trained with, was deemed no longer a security risk.

Chapter 3

TRAINING AND DESPATCH

EACH SMALL GROUP, DESIGNATED A 'PARTY', OF TRAINEE AGENTS HAD A 'conducting' member of staff with them at all times. As time went on, this was sometimes an agent, returned from the field, who had relevant experience and was therefore well-placed to monitor his or her charges. In the company of their conducting member of staff, an F Section party (typically six to ten, but sometimes up to 17 or 18 trainees) would be taken to Guildford in Surrey, 40 miles south-west of London. This journey was usually by train and at Guildford station a covered army truck waited. Discouraged from looking out from the truck, the trainees then had to endure a bumpy and twisting drive for anything between one and two hours before they arrived at a large manor house, set in extensive wooded grounds and closely guarded by armed Field Security Police of the British Army's Intelligence Corps. All passes were scrupulously checked at the entrance.

The trainees did not know it, but their journey had been a deliberately circuitous one, encouraging them to believe their destination was something like 30 miles from where the lorry had picked them up at the station. Designed to prevent them knowing exactly where their training establishment was, this was another ploy used against the possibility that a trainee might later be found unsuitable. In reality, only a short journey of 10 minutes from Guildford station would have taken them up and out of the town along the Farnham road, which followed the Hog's Back ridge of high ground. Off the main road and downhill in the small hamlet of Wanborough lay the trainees' home for the next two or three weeks, Wanborough Manor.

Requisitioned for use as Special Training School (STS) 5, one of SOE's Preliminary Schools, Wanborough Manor was a large country house taken over by the British government soon after war broke out. So many such properties were used as Special Training Schools that it was jokingly said that SOE stood for 'Stately 'Omes of England'. Substantial, though not in the grand class of some other SOE acquisitions, the Manor was built in 1527 and boasted an outdoor swimming pool and numerous barns (the largest had been built in or shortly after 1388 for the Cistercian monks of Waverley Abbey) and stables which were useful for SOE's training and storage needs. The tiny but beautiful 13th century church and graveyard of Saint Bartholomew, mentioned in the Domesday Book and said to be the smallest church in the county, was immediately adjacent and connected to the Manor and available for those trainees who were regular worshippers. A memorial plaque in the church commemorates the agents trained at Wanborough.

STS 5, Wanborough Manor, near Guildford in Surrey. Photo: author's coll.

The new arrivals were met by the commandant, originally Major Douglas Larder and later, from June 1941, Major Roger de Wesselow, a very proper and disciplined former officer of the Coldstream Guards, a personal friend of Sir Charles Hambro, and a keen horse racing enthusiast. The staff were tough, capable instructors, mostly sergeants, assisted by other soldiers and orderlies for day-to-day duties. The Manor's perimeter was constantly patrolled by the Field Security Police and was in an area off-limits to all civilians so that the nascent agents could receive their initial training under the cloak of secrecy. In theory, neither staff nor students were permitted outside the compound unless on exercises and under escort, and leave was only granted in exceptional circumstances. But in practice and as the courses progressed, spare time was given and trips were permitted into Guildford, thereby negating the need for measures taken to disguise the Manor's whereabouts when the trainees first arrived. Letters home were still allowed, but were censored. The trainee was not permitted to say or speculate exactly where he or she was, or what they were doing, and relatives and friends could write only via an anonymous P.O. Box number in London.

A typical day at Wanborough began at 06:00 with a hot drink and biscuit. An hour's physical exercise followed, rewarded by breakfast in the common Mess. The full day then consisted of a mixture of lectures by specialists such as intelligence officers, sappers, ordnance experts, and detectives from Scotland Yard. Theory was tested by practical exercises in the grounds of the Manor which included two small quarries, one being used for hand grenade practice and the other as a shooting range, suitable for machine guns as well as pistols. Trainees were told how they would be issued with a pistol if and when sent to France, and were expected to aim by pointing it like a finger from the middle of the body and squeezing off two shots as rapidly as possible in the classic 'double tap' technique. This was in order to deliver, from any position and in any light, even in the dark, maximum stopping power as quickly as possible into the vulnerable part of an enemy's body, the area from his groin to the top of his head. If there were no other threat to be dealt with, two more shots would make absolutely certain of finishing the victim off. The student agents also learned use of the mass-produced Sten gun, supplied in great numbers to resistance forces thanks to its uncomplicated design and cheap cost of manufacture.

There were initial courses in map reading and sabotage, basic sending and receiving in Morse code, unarmed combat, and weapons training. Each subject was first explained by lecturers, and then came the practical experience. The introduction to plastic explosive included advice to keep it about the person where body warmth would soften it and make it easier to mould onto the object to be destroyed. It could be dropped, kicked, and heated without anything happening. But detonators, unlike plastic explosive, were very temperamental and had to be handled carefully. Some of them, made of mercury fulminate, could not be carried in the hand because even the heat of the body could explode them. It was not unknown for trainees to lose hands or fingers blown off through incautious handling. It was stressed that it was unwise to run when carrying detonators, because if you tripped and fell, it would probably be the last thing you did. In the Manor's grounds the trainees practiced setting charges to destroy a short stretch of railway track, receiving the critical advice never to run away having laid a charge in case one tripped after only a step or two and consequently went up with the target. There were different instructions on blowing bridges, dams, or transformers and using plastic explosive or amatol, the latter being another explosive which consisted of a mixture of TNT and ammonium nitrate.

Assault courses and more exercises were designed to challenge and improve physical endurance, helped by Major de Wesselow who, although over 50 years of age, rarely missed setting the pace for the daily run of the trainee agents along the nearby Hog's Back ridge. Despite the Commandant's authoritarian leanings, at least one former agent remembers that the daily run sometimes continued unofficially along the road that led to the local pub. Dependent upon the season, a dip in the open-air swimming pool often rounded off the day before a hot bath and dinner, where officers and sergeants, instructors and staff, mixed freely and enjoyed a good standard of food. Pleasant evenings were often spent in the school's bar where, as in the Mess, there was no rank distinction and everyone seemed kind, welcoming and helpful. The songs of the popular French singer Charles Trénet were frequently heard on the gramophone, F Section's favourite being *'Je tire ma révérence et m'en vais au hasard sur les routes de France, de France et de Navarre….'*

Yet even in the bar, the trainees were being closely, if unobtrusively, observed. For the staff were noting not only their students' grasp of the material being taught, but also their character traits and actions. This included an assessment of behaviour under the influence of alcohol and the conviviality of the bar. The ability to hold one's drink, or an inclination to become indiscreet, were among the details included in de Wesselow's weekly report on the group, backed up by his own regular trips up to London or visits by the Orchard Court staff to Wanborough. At the very end of the day, the beds were comfortable, but their dormitory sleeping quarters proved to be yet another testing ground, bugged to discover whether the students talked in their sleep - and if so, in what language? They would similarly be woken roughly in the middle of the night in order to test whether their first, irritable, words were in French or English. And if that were not enough, there were sometimes night exercises when a group would have to slip out, lay dummy charges on a railway line some miles away, and return to Wanborough, undetected, before dawn.

From July 1943, STS 5's preliminary assessment of trainees at Wanborough Manor was replaced by a more scientific method, implemented by a Students' Assessment Board based at STS 7, Winterfold, near to Cranleigh in Surrey. A standard assessment template was created, using three general headings:

I. <u>General Agent Grading</u>

A	Outstanding
B	Good
C+	Above Average
C	Average
C-	Below Average
D	Low, but Pass
F	Fail

II. <u>Intelligence Rating</u>

1		Mentally Dull
2	}	
3	}	Intermediate Ratings
4	}	
5		Average Intelligence
6	}	
7	}	Intermediate Ratings
8	}	
9		Superior Intelligence

III. <u>Aptitude Gradings</u>

a) Morse	Good pass
	Average Pass
	Fail
b) Mechanical	Good
	Aptitude Average
	Poor
c) Instructional	Good
	Ability Average
	Poor

Aptitude gradings were purely technical assessments and took no account of the student's personality or general intelligence. In conclusion, there would be a few sentences of summary comments under the heading 'Remarks', any comment from F Section headquarters and a decision by STS HQ's Group A commandant as to which STS the trainee, after a week's leave, would now go for paramilitary training.

STS 7, Winterfold, near Cranleigh in Surrey. Photo: author, courtesy of Tony Hampton.

The Group A Paramilitary Schools were located in and around Arisaig, on the west coast of the county of Inverness-shire in the highlands of Scotland. This element of the training syllabus was originally planned to last three weeks, but as the war progressed, so did the length of the course until some trainees underwent up to five weeks' instruction. Remote from civilisation, these establishments were the result of one of Brigadier Gubbins's early priorities when he joined SOE, to set up the training schools that would take over after initial assessment and basic instruction. In the early months of 1941 he had quickly achieved his aim. Not too distant from his own family links with the Isle of Mull, he had obtained use of an extensive area in and around Arisaig, which he knew well. This district could only be approached by one road, by a single-track railway, or by water. So rugged and desolate was it that it was known as the Highlands of the Highlands and during the Second World War an extensive zone west of Fort William became a Special Protected Area, off limits to the general public other than the local residents who had special passes and could be relied upon not to talk.

Some 500 miles north from London, via Glasgow and Fort William, the area was perfect for Gubbins's paramilitary schools and he secured the use of ten houses and shooting lodges. Arisaig House became the centre for SOE's network of training establishments in the area and the other properties used were Rhubana Lodge, Meoble Lodge, Swordland, Inverie House, Glaschollie, Garramor House, Camusdarrach, Traigh House and Morar Lodge. Most of the area is wild, mountainous and exceptionally lonely and as such, was ideally suited to SOE's purposes.

The trainees learned to make and throw Molotov cocktail bombs on the shores of Loch Morar and they paddled out onto it in canoes to attach limpet mines to steel plates sunk in the water, simulating ship sabotage. Sabotage techniques on land, for both industrial and railway targets, were even more crucial, demolition and explosives training being high priorities on the syllabus of the Group A schools. Laying dummy charges and fog signals, rail sabotage was carried out with the cooperation of the West Highland Line, who also arranged for the would-be agents to visit the end of the line at Mallaig where they were given the chance to drive, and become familiar, with the construction of a large steam locomotive. They became more familiar with the different types of explosive, SOE's original plastic explosive being a nitro-glycerine based substance called 808 which, ironically, was the invention of Alfred Nobel, founder of the Nobel Peace Prize. It had a peculiar smell of almonds, but unless over-heated, was very flexible and could easily be cut and shaped. It was later replaced by RDX, a more powerful plastic explosive and without the tell-tale aroma. SOE called it PE, or 'plastique'. To preserve supplies of this valuable explosive, only gelignite was used in training.

A typical sabotage exercise at Arisaig might involve six or so trainees given the task of setting explosives on a railway engine in broad daylight. They would be given the target's map reference, a briefing, and were then left to plan and carry out the attack. Two agents would approach the target from one direction, two more from another, and the other couple from a third. Courses had to be plotted beforehand so that they could keep out of sight of enemy guards and patrols, roles played with much enthusiasm by the instructors who were always vigilant and ready to advise when things went wrong. The scheme would usually entail a lengthy cross-country approach, during which the saboteurs would follow the lie of the land, using whatever cover there was and keeping out of sight of all high ground where watchers might have been posted. After placing the charge on the engine, equally important was a successful escape.

Techniques that are today the staple diet of special forces around the world were developed and perfected – cross-country map reading by day and night, how to set an ambush or storm a house. The six acres of wild gardens enjoyed by Garramor House, just a few minutes' walk from the famous white sandy beaches of Loch Morar with their breath-taking views of the islands of Eigg, Rum, Muck and Skye, were home to a special shooting range. One of the first of its kind, it had houses whose doors opened and closed while dummy targets suddenly sprang out on pulleys from all angles, testing the trainee's reflexes and instincts of whether to open fire or not. There they learned to handle arms and ammunition without thinking, practicing how to assemble, dismantle and shoot a variety of rifles, pistols, PIATs, Sten and Bren guns, the weapons most often dropped to the *Résistance*, and how to instruct others in their use. For occasions when a gun was inappropriate, they extended their knowledge of unarmed combat, including, when necessary, that of silent killing. This black art had been perfected by two of SOE's earliest trainers in Scotland, Major Fairbairn, a former Shanghai police officer, and his close colleague Captain Sykes, whom Fairbairn had known in Shanghai. Dubbed "The Heavenly Twins", they were to design the famed Fairbairn-Sykes double-edged commando knife, still today in widespread use throughout the world. Other instructors were usually Army personnel, including many Highlanders. One such was Gavin Maxwell, later to become a well-respected writer and author of the acclaimed book 'Ring of Bright Water'.

The rugged, but beautiful, landscape of the area around Loch Morar was home to SOE's paramilitary training establishments. Photo: author's coll.

No distinction was made between the sexes. Men and women trainees alike trekked over the rough country, often in appalling weather, wading through cold rushing streams and creeping through the heather to hide from the other groups of trainees sent out in patrols to hunt for them. One agent, John Goldsmith, would describe his paramilitary school as the place where 'we played deadly forms of Boy Scout games' and 'a cross between going back to school and staying in a series of first-class hotels where shooting, hunting and even fishing were free'. But the outdoor, aggressive, life proved a severe test of an agent's potential and up to a third of the trainees on each course were found lacking and regretfully advised that their training was at an end. For women to undergo this training in preparation for roles as courier or radio operator was unprecedented and their eventual contribution on active service in the field was not made public until some time after the war had ended, when it was still considered controversial. To an instructor, or an outsider, those men and women trainees whose nerve and stamina had survived the Group A schools were now demonstrably tougher and more self-confident. This strengthening of self-confidence in a trainee's ability was very much needed for the usual next phase of training, short in duration, but as much a test as anything in the entire syllabus – parachute training.

STS 51a Dunham House. Photo: Tony and Halina McDonald.

SOE's parachute course involved trainees being lodged in one of two large houses near Manchester: Dunham House, STS 51a, at Altrincham or Fulshaw Hall, STS 51b, at Wilmslow.

Both were conveniently located for access to the nearby RAF aerodrome at Ringway known to SOE as STS 51 and now Manchester International Airport. Four or five jumps were required, including one at night and one with a leg bag attached, useful for gaining a second or so's notice of hitting the ground in the dark. It was not unusual for a sizeable majority of each group of trainees to have never flown before and there were isolated instances of agents flatly refusing to take the course. Only if their other ability and promise outweighed this refusal did they continue and receive the option of a sea-borne or aircraft landing.

The course commenced with instruction on the ground. The trainees learned, from an aircraft fuselage mock-up, how to jump from a hatch in the floor of the aircraft and how to land and roll safely. A first jump was normally made from a tethered balloon in Tatton Park, an experience which many found more challenging than their first jump from an aircraft, since the ground appeared unnervingly close. They were then taken to RAF Ringway where they watched other trainee parachutists and familiarised themselves with the layout of their dropping aircraft. This was normally a lumbering obsolete bomber, the twin-engined Whitley, a type used by the RAF's Special Duties squadrons for dropping SOE agents in the organisation's early days.

Trainees receiving ground instruction at Ringway. Photos: author's coll.

The ageing Whitley was used at Ringway by STS 51. Photo: author's coll.

Returning to their accommodation after this observation of others, a nervous night would then be spent before a return to Ringway the next day for the real thing. Any remaining fears were not eased by the instructors who, vastly-experienced, frequently had a macabre disregard for the occasional accidents that occurred. Parachuting was, they declared, 'the only wonderful sensation that the opposite sex can't give you' and they were fond of quipping, 'if your parachute doesn't open, report to the stores and you'll get another'. The Whitley would climb to an altitude of around 1,000 feet, and head towards the drop zone of either Tatton Park or Dunham Massey Hall. The instructor announced three minutes to the jump and the dispatcher moved to the open hatch in the fuselage floor. The instructor was to be the first to go and positioned himself, seated on the edge of the hatch with his feet hanging down into space while the trainees lined up in pairs behind him. The dispatcher shouted "Action Stations!" quickly followed by a downward sweep of his arm and the cry 'number one, GO'. The instructor disappeared as the dispatcher continued 'number two, GO' and the trainees followed in their turn. There were only seconds to wait until a sharp tug on the shoulders announced that the static line had done its work and jerked open the parachute. There was little time to admire the scenery as the ground soon rushed up to meet the trainees who then had put their training into practice, bending knees and rolling on landing. All being well, the trainees would then be able to stand and roll up their parachute before returning to Ringway for another two or three more daylight jumps culminating, if time and conditions allowed, in a night jump. The course completed, the trainees could expect to receive their prized uniform parachute wings and were then sent back to London. There, at SOE headquarters, progress to date was reviewed and, in preparation for the next stage of training, assessment made as to whether the trainee was to become an organiser, assistant organiser, radio operator, sabotage specialist, or courier.

Tethered balloons were used for practice jumps into Tatton Park before the real thing. Photos: author's and R.A. Bridgeford coll.

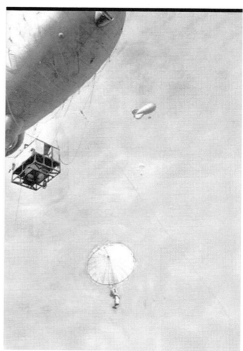

Those who were viewed as potential radio (W/T) operators, colloquially known as 'pianists' within SOE, were required to undertake an intensive course at the wireless-training school, STS 52, at Thame Park in Oxfordshire, another stately home and hidden from view four miles off the London to Oxford road, some 14 miles from the famous university town. Set in some of the oldest enclosed parkland in England, Thame Park had a long and remarkable history. The main part of the house was Georgian, though the oldest part dated from the 13th century and was once part of a Cistercian abbey, still possessing arched cloisters. The entire estate included over a thousand acres of park and farmland with a seven-acre lake and a sunken rose garden and it was in this impressive setting that SOE's trainee radio operators learned their dangerous trade – dangerous since the wastage rate of operators was high, thanks to the ability of the Germans to detect their transmissions, locate and catch the operator. A shortage of trained W/T personnel was a permanent problem for SOE, exacerbated by the role requiring not only coding and transmitting expertise, but also a particular type of character, since operators often worked in isolation and had little opportunity for contact with others.

STS 52 at Thame Park in Oxfordshire and a typical W/T set hidden in a suitcase.
Photos: Oxfordshire County Council and author's coll..

CHAPTER 3 – TRAINING AND DESPATCH

Up until 1942, SOE was dependent upon SIS (MI6) for communications with its agents abroad. This changed with the opening of two signals stations not far from Thame Park, at Grendon Underwood and Poundon in Buckinghamshire, and the development of codes and ciphers solely for SOE use. Hand in hand with this went Thame Park's training programme which was anything from six to 12 weeks in duration, dependent upon the trainee's previous experience in radio work, though several breaks were involved. The house offered a fine library, the singing of songs by the piano and table tennis. There was also the opportunity to go to the cinema and to dances in the locality, a marked relaxation after the earlier stages of training. Several different country sections of SOE trained there simultaneously, but were kept strictly segregated.

The days at Thame Park were crammed with continuous instruction in codes and the operation of short wave radio transmitter/receivers, capable of reaching up to 500 miles. The set weighed in at a hefty 30 pounds or so, but fitted neatly into an innocuous two-foot long suitcase. A vital addition to be carried separately was the crystals that fitted to the set and set the wavelength for transmissions.

W/T operators learned that in towns it might take the Germans as little as 30 minutes to discover where a transceiver was being used. Where possible, operators were therefore recommended to work in isolated areas and were under strict instructions to transmit short, concise messages, at irregular intervals, at various wavelengths and from various places. In theory, the circuit organiser would be responsible for coding and decoding his own messages and the W/T operator responsible only for transmitting or receiving them. In practice, however, it was recognised and accepted that the W/T operator often also undertook coding. Ideally, the same location ought not to be used on two consecutive occasions, but this meant that either the operator had to move his set from house to house, or have several sets permanently sited in the different locations. The former option was highly dangerous, since if stopped at a checkpoint, an operator would stand no chance of explaining away the transceiver set in his suitcase. The alternative, however, involved the operator having to be supplied with several sets and this took some time to achieve. Keeping transmissions as brief as possible was in order to give the least possible chance of detection to the Germans' radio interception service, the *Funk-Horchdienst*.[1] If a lengthy message were necessary, it had to be sent on two or more schedules ('skeds') of which each operator normally had three or four a week. A schedule was the time slot when Home Station back in England would be listening on the operator's frequency.

Power for the W/T set could come from two sources. Batteries had the disadvantage of needing recharging, but enabled use of a set in the countryside where mains power might not be available. The electric mains were more reliable, but since electricity consumption would be metered, agents had to learn how to tap the mains before the meter. If practicable, it was also recommended that a guard should keep watch outside. It was stressed that it could be dangerous for an operator to be seen with his or her organiser, and that it was

---

1   By late 1943, SOE headquarters were to decree that transmissions were not to exceed five minutes, and preferably much less, in order to avoid the Germans' detection services.

best to communicate by 'cut-outs', intermediaries whose only job was to act as couriers, carrying messages from one agent to another. This also helped with other security rules for W/T operators who were warned of the danger of over-enthusiasm and instructed that they should not attempt to find out more about the circuit than they were told, not know more than one or two members and not undertake other subversive activity.

If the worst came to the worst and a W/T operator were arrested, the trainees gathered that they could expect not to be executed immediately, but that instead, attempts would be made by the enemy to 'persuade' them to reveal their W/T plan so that their set could be operated back to England, either by the W/T operator under duress, or by German personnel. To guard against such an eventuality, radio operators had to pre-arrange 'security checks' before they left England, words or phrases that could be omitted from messages in order to alert Home Station if all were not well. Unfortunately, agents were prone to forgetting to include their security checks, to the extent that on occasions SOE reminded and chastised agents for forgetting the checks. This had disastrous consequences in a number of instances where the Germans <u>had</u> captured agents and sets and the enemy were consequently alerted, by SOE's naivety, to the omission of the checks. The consequences for the captured operator could be fatal.

Long-range transmissions were normally practiced by two exercises, called 'schemes', each a week or so long, from somewhere in Scotland, Wales or the north of England where the trainee would have had to find lodgings and, without attracting the local authorities, transmit messages every day back to Thame where they were scrutinised carefully for accuracy. The local civil and military police were sometimes tipped off and given details that enabled them to look for and, if possible, to follow and arrest trainees carrying out these exercises.

Originally, trainee wireless operators had received security training during their stay at Thame Park, sometimes at nearby Grendon Underwood. But after many early losses of operators in France, something more was clearly needed and so, from the spring of 1942, wireless operator trainees were sent for more extensive security training at one of the finishing schools at Beaulieu (see below). Though this specialised training increased the security awareness of radio operators, of all agents they nevertheless remained most at risk of detection and capture and at one time their average survival rate in France was calculated at only three months. Even after security training they were prone to becoming careless when their enforced isolation in the field drove them to become sloppy and take risks. In addition, the Germans knew that a wireless operator, while being technically vulnerable to detection, could also prove to be the key to uncovering an entire circuit. They knew that the operator would at least be in touch with the circuit organiser and possibly, as the circuit's 'post-box', with several others.

One of the most important elements of an agent's training usually then came next – a Group B Finishing School at Beaulieu in Hampshire. The course there was located on the ancestral estate of the Lords Montagu in the New Forest, where the trainees were lodged in houses and cottages in the grounds. Even with barbed wire fences, and temporary wartime building additions, it was a beautiful place, and many agents later remembered Beaulieu as an enchanted setting, despite the intense concentration and hard work that was demanded of them. It was certainly a pleasant experience compared to the harsh conditions that, dependent upon the season, could be encountered at the Group A schools in the Highlands of Scotland.

Depending on the train timetables, agents could be sent to the mainline stations of Southampton or Brockenhurst, but the slow, stopping service would deposit trainees at Beaulieu Road Station, nearest to their goal and from where transport would be waiting to take them the final four miles. On arrival they were allocated to one of a series of twelve houses, of differing sizes, but mostly built on the estate for friends of Lord Montagu in the early 1900's. The training staff lived in one of these, a large house named The Rings (STS 31) and were commanded by Colonel Frank Spooner. His lecturers and instructors were as varied and eclectic a group as the agents themselves, and included many talented individuals later to gain fame, or infamy. Hardy Amies, the Queen's future couturier, was one, and Kim Philby, eventually to find notoriety when discovered to be a Soviet double agent, was another before he transferred to SIS. A number of former Scotland Yard officers found themselves instructing alongside erstwhile adversaries from the 'trades' of burglary, safe-cracking etc, and all were supported by a sprinkling of 'resting' agents already returned from France who could speak from experience in the field. Beaulieu's syllabus was divided into five sections, each with its own department responsible for delivering the instructions. These were:

Department A – agent techniques, clandestine life and organisation, personal security, communications methods and the use of sub-agents.
Department B – exercises to test the instruction from Department A.
Department C – enemy forces, including the Vichy French as well as the Germans.
Department D – clandestine propaganda, both factual and fictitious.
Department E – use of secret codes, ciphers and inks.

Department A's training included the all-important element of taking on a false identity by assuming a new name, fabricating a life to support the name, perhaps adopting a disguise, and then learning how to live with this false identity under enemy occupation. The requirements of day-to-day living in German-occupied or Vichy France could be new, even to those who had grown up in the country. Very few would be familiar with the ration books used when making purchases, when and how to show their identity papers when challenged, how to pass through a snap control at a rail station. Trainees could expect to be required to produce, in addition to an identity card, a work permit, a ration card, a tobacco card, a permit if in a coastal or frontier zone, as well as, for males of military service age, demobilisation papers and a medical certificate establishing exemption from forced labour in Germany. Each forgery of these papers in the possession of an agent had to be the up-to-date official form, correctly signed and stamped. French Section agent John Goldsmith remembered:

'There was so much to pick up since my last visit to France in 1938…facts about politics; what it was practical to ask for in the shops; who the latest film stars and what the songs of the moment were'. And such things as the *jour sans,* the days on which spirits were not available, and asking for a vermouth cassis in a café instead of ordering ersatz coffee or a lemonade could mark you more certainly than carrying forged papers.'

Expert interrogators would then question the students to see what holes might be found in their stories. Any mistake would be pointed out, and the trainee reminded that a similar slip in France could be expected to lead to torture and death.

It was stressed that survival depended on remembering the details. From Department C trainees had to learn the wide range of uniforms and ranks of the enemy's military and intelligence forces that could be encountered in France, especially those that might be looking for the agent. These forces included not just the Germans, but also the Vichy French who operated numerous armed police and paramilitary organisations. A country *gendarme* would rarely pose any great threat and, indeed, could often be relied upon to help or take part in resistance. But the *Milice*, a volunteer paramilitary organisation of French fascists, were always dangerous and frequently operated alongside the Germans. Their agents and informers, local French people with an eye to gaining advantage from the occupier, were always in a very small and generally-despised minority. Yet they represented one of the greatest threats to an agent, given their local knowledge and their greater ability than the Germans to detect subtle differences in language and behaviour.

If captured, an agent was expected to stay silent, no matter how harsh the interrogation, for 48 hours. This would give some time for a warning to reach all the people who had been in contact with him or her to move house and cover their tracks. Officers from the Intelligence Corps normally undertook the interrogation sessions, lasting up to five hours, that came as close to the real thing as possible without involving actual physical torture. Trainees were threatened, screamed at, pushed around, kept standing under bright lights and questioned repeatedly without respite. They also received unsettling instruction on exactly how vicious and unscrupulous the German secret police and intelligence forces were expected to be. SOE rightly assumed that their agents, even if members of the British armed forces, and perhaps even in uniform, would receive little mercy if captured, and would fall outside the protection of the Geneva Conventions and the normal arrangements for POWs.

One aspect of the course covered survival techniques and was run by Captain William 'Nobby' Clark, an expert instructor in living off the land and field craft. A large man with a ruddy complexion, he had risen through the ranks of the regular army and had served in the First World War before becoming a gamekeeper on the royal estate at Sandringham in Norfolk. From other instructors equally well-versed in their specific areas of expertise, trainees learned how to write messages in invisible ink and how to search people properly, being warned that some collaborators did not carry written messages on paper, but on their bodies instead. They learned how to make contacts in the field, set up safe houses and mail drops and to pass messages surreptitiously in public places.

In the event that an agent were suspected by the enemy, he or she had to become adept at spotting and shaking off a pursuer when being followed. Another course showed how to locate and prepare suitable landing and dropping grounds for the reception of arms and other agents. In one of the smaller houses, set in Beaulieu's woods, trainees were taught some particularly useful methods of opening handcuffs, picking locks, and breaking safes. The instructors were in uniform, but some were known to have questionable peacetime backgrounds.

The drill was taught for entering a public establishment such as a restaurant or bar. Firstly, the agent should take a good look around outside, just in case there were Gestapo, other Germans or French *Milice* about. On entering, it was preferable to choose a table facing the door, or the foyer, so as to obtain the best possible view of all that was going on, and who came and went. It was also advisable to sit with one's back against a wall, so that one could not be watched or surprised from behind. Possible escape routes also had to be identified in advance and as quickly as possible, in case of trouble. Options should include windows, the waiters' entrance to the kitchens, the toilets etc. Identity cards and other similar documentation was to be carried at all times in case of spot checks, without them, an agent would attract suspicion and might have to accompany a policeman, or worse, to his or her house or hotel to pick up the documentation. That would only serve to give away more information, namely the place where the agent lived. It was important, too, to have ready a simple, and preferably verifiable, excuse for being in a particular place at a particular time, so that the agent could plausibly explain where he/she was going, and why.

Lectures included detailed briefings on the different political groupings among the French and the trainees were taught how to organise, nurture, arm and supply a resistance group. While controversial and often attracting criticism, SOE's policy was to ignore politics in general and to simply support whoever had the most potential for harming the enemy. In France, this meant that agents often had a sensitive role to play between communist and Gaullist *Résistance* groups who had very different long-term objectives. But at least it was acceptable to support both. Elsewhere, choices had to be made and meant, for example, that in Yugoslavia, SOE supported Tito's communist partisans and not the monarchy, while in neighbouring Greece they backed the exiled king rather than the communists. In northern Italy, as will be seen in the story of Captain Ronald Taylor, the position among the different partisan groups was particularly complicated, with competing political and territorial aims.

Beaulieu's training was also tested by 'schemes'. The 36 hours' scheme was often in one of the nearby coastal towns or cities of Southampton, Bournemouth or Portsmouth and involved the agent having to carry out some act of sabotage or intelligence gathering in a closely-guarded area. An overnight stay was involved and the local police and Field Security units, on alert, had to be thrown off. If they weren't, the exercise would also involve arrest and interrogation and the trainee had to rely on their cover story or attempt to escape. Only as a last resort could they telephone a special number in order to be bailed out by the SOE staff. In his book 'Xavier', Richard Heslop, a highly-successful French Section agent, described one of the exercises:

'We were sent on an exercise to Bournemouth to test out our training on passing messages, remembering code introductions, and using methods to make certain one was not being followed. It was a simple exercise really, but important. If I were told that my headquarters would be a small hotel, then I would have to walk through the town to deliver a message to a man in another hotel. The first thing I said to him had to be the phrase which would identify myself correctly, and I had to memorize the actual message. He would identify himself by using another introductory phrase, and if I did not get the correct reply, then I must walk away. I saw my man and, to avoid being followed, used all the tricks that later were to become second nature to me. When I came out of my hotel I walked a little way down the street, suddenly fumbled in my pocket as though I had forgotten something, and then turned around quickly and returned to the hotel. That enabled me to see who was on both pavements and walking towards me. The next time I came out I checked to see that none of these people were still about. It was essential to re-enter the hotel, otherwise you tipped the trained fellow that you were suspicious.'

'Other methods we were taught were simple and effective. For instance, if you knew you were being followed, you could keep an eye open for a bus and hop on it at the last moment, which normally meant that the follower would not have a chance to catch up. Just to make certain, you hopped off and caught a bus going in another direction. Or you could walk into a busy store like, say, Selfridges, take a lift up three flights, walk up two more, take a lift down four, and then walk out of a back door. That got rid of most people. Another trick was to choose a gentlemen's lavatory with an exit and an entry. You would walk in a normal way, wait a couple of minutes and then walk out the same way you went in. Simple but effective.'

The '96 hours' scheme' came at the very end of the course, was much more complex, and involved travelling to and from a more distant city in England. Sometimes alone, sometimes in a small group of two or three, trainee agents were given a specific, often criminal, task such as planting explosives in a factory or on a railway line, or reconnoitring a military facility Normally, several contacts had to be made and a variety of targets reconnoitred or attacked.

Again, Heslop recalled:

'My last exercise, almost a passing out examination, was to Nottingham. I was told that I must go there in civvies, without any identity cards, get into a forbidden zone, gather what information I could, and return to Beaulieu. I invented a cover story, set off, and, without any trouble at all, evaded guards at the factory where I was to ferret out production details and so on.'

Upon completion of their Group B Finishing School training, agents were cleared for service in France, subject to any final training (especially for circuit leaders) for an additional expertise. Such instruction was delivered by the Group C Operational Schools, such as STS 40, at Howbury Hall near Bedford, which ran a course covering the arranging of Reception Committees for aircraft landings or parachute drops, and STS 17 at Brickendonbury, Hertford, which taught industrial sabotage.

STS 40, Howbury Hall and (right)
STS 17, Brickendonbury.
Photos: author's coll.

By this programme of instruction, the Special Training Schools imbued the trainee with the aggression, confidence, self-control and caution that were required for survival in the field. Such was the desperate need to despatch agents at critical times of the war that elements of the training would be cut out, or accelerated, with potentially-tragic consequences for an agent. The schools' findings on the suitability of an agent could also be over-ridden on the gut feeling of a senior officer, such as Buckmaster, if the need were pressing – sometimes with disastrous implications, but also, on occasion, with a surprising degree of prescience.

The final briefing for a French Section agent included the all-important cover story and assumed identity. If a different profession were involved, this could involve basic job training, but generally the job assigned to the false identity matched with what an agent already had experience of. Final instruction was received in the tiniest of details that SOE continually collected to allow an agent to operate as unobtrusively as possible. This included any recent changes in documents needed and the conditions of daily life, including the enemy's latest regulations about travel, curfew and work. Much of this information came from refugees or escapers from France, from messages radioed back, and from those agents returning from a first tour of duty in the field.

Civilian 'French' clothes came from a small company in London run by a Jewish refugee from Austria, originally contracted by SOE to collect second-hand continental clothes and personal effects such as wallets, watches and suitcases from synagogues and refugee centres. As such original items became scarce, the company had expanded into making clothes to order and to their own continental fashion designs. An agent would visit the company's discreet workshop near Oxford Circus for fittings by a team of tailors and seamstresses. Even the smallest incorrect detail, such as the way a label was stitched, could on inspection betray an agent. Anything that was newly-made had to be 'worn in' so that the agent would not look expensively-dressed and so arouse suspicion of black-marketeering.

A full medical check-up included an inspection for dental work that had not been performed in the continental manner. Any tell-tale British-style fillings, for example, meant a potentially-painful visit to an inconspicuous French dentist in Maddox Street. A French-style haircut completed the picture and agents were then photographed for their false identity cards, expertly forged along with their other documents at SOE's own directly-staffed establishment.

At some point, a French Section agent about to depart England would have a brief interview with the head of the Section. A tall man, with a gentle manner, Major (later Colonel) Maurice Buckmaster was thought by some to have been a little naïve for a secret service chief, and to have lacked the ruthlessness that one might have expected. But no-one ever questioned his dedication to the job, he was acutely aware of the importance and value of his agents and he cared about them deeply. He made a habit of presenting agents, as they were about to leave for the field, with a personal gift such as gold cuff-links or a gold compact or brooch. These naturally had no British markings, but would remind the agent he or she was not forgotten back at headquarters. More practically, the gift could also be sold if an agent were short of money.

Lastly, the agent would have had a sobering interview about their will, next of kin and contacts in the event of their death. This was usually conducted by a formidable woman in the uniform of the WAAF, Vera Atkins. Nominally French Section's Intelligence Officer and personal assistant to Buckmaster, Atkins was considered by many to be the real power in the Section. Of a Romanian father and a British mother, she had been born Vera Maria Rosenberg in Bucharest and had studied modern languages at the Sorbonne. She returned to England when France was invaded in May 1940 and joined SOE in February 1941 where her responsibilities included interviewing recruits, organising their training, creating cover stories and planning agent receptions in France. Like Buckmaster, she was indefatigable and was always immaculate, with not a hair out of place. Her presence was found formidable by many, but intimidating by some and she could cow even the most ebullient agent with a caustic remark and an icy glare. But she made a point of personally seeing as many as possible of those leaving for France, making arrangements for letters to be sent to relatives while the agents were out of touch, taking charge of personal possessions left behind, and briefing them on what to expect once they landed. Atkins was also renowned, and occasionally later blessed, for the odds and sods of daily French life that she collected, from only she knew where, to help equip agents. These included photos of supposed friends and relatives, apparently genuine receipts from French shops, letters with seemingly valid postal franks from other cities, Métro tickets, etc. Even if they were never inspected, these small additions boosted an agent's confidence by strengthening the impression that French Section knew their job.

With the briefing completed, the agent was at last ready to become one of what Buckmaster was later to describe as F Section's 'unofficial ambassadors of the free world'. If feasible, agents were permitted home leave, but with strict instructions to say nothing to friends or relatives about the work for which they were now ready. French Section agents then faced a variety of methods for their insertion into enemy-occupied France. Although some (such as Captain Edward Zeff) were landed by submarine, or by boat on deserted stretches of the enemy-guarded coast, some 90% of agents who were delivered to France went by air. Flights were normally limited to only the five or six nights either side of a full moon, when visibility was good enough for accurate navigation and identification of landing grounds (LGs) and drop zones DZs). That was the theory. In practice, and especially in the winter months, poor weather conditions would jeopardise these 'moon periods' and in reality there were often only very few nights each month that were suitable for operations.

If the insertion were to be via a landing ground, the ubiquitous Westland Lysander was usually the aircraft used by the RAF's Special Duties squadrons. Despite its small size, the single-engined Lysander could carry one agent comfortably, two at a pinch and very occasionally three at a very tight squeeze. Its immensely strong and forgiving undercarriage, together with a remarkable short take off and landing ability, made it ideal for the rough and ready airstrips of the *résistants* and if all went smoothly, agents could be set down and picked up in just three minutes on the ground. One drawback was the Lysander's restricted range, but this was overcome by an additional fuel tank and use of the Fighter Command airfield at Tangmere, near Chichester on the south coast of England, as a forward operating base. This avoided the need to use up precious fuel, since the Special Duties squadrons' home base was RAF Tempsford in Bedfordshire, 120 miles from the southern coast. Twin-engined Lockheed Hudsons had greater range and were also available for landings, but required a much longer airstrip and so were reserved for operations where groups of personnel had to be delivered or brought out.

The alternative to a landing by Lysander or Hudson was to parachute, as taught to most French Section agents at RAF Ringway and as already described above. Operational drops were generally from just 500 or 600 feet, with the aircraft flying at a relatively sedate 100-120 miles an hour, and were flown to France from RAF Tempsford (the very earliest operations were flown from RAF Newmarket) using the RAF's Special Duties squadrons'

Whitley, Hudson, Halifax and Stirling aircraft, augmented by the USAAF's B-24 Liberators and C-47 Skytrains, the latter being better known by their civilian name, the DC-3 Dakota. This was not a method for the faint-hearted and several agents flatly refused the option, or were otherwise prevented from jumping by injury or insufficient time to undertake the Ringway training. Those who did, however, were entitled, if they returned, to wear their 'jump' wings on the left breast of their uniform, denoting that they had made an operational jump behind enemy lines. Similar SOE parachute training schools to Ringway were operated for Europe-bound agents near Algiers (after the Allied landings in north Africa had taken place) and at Ramat David in Palestine, now Israel. Of the four blue plaque recipients, Captain Michael Trotobas, Lieutenant Jacqueline Nearne and Captain Ronald Taylor were delivered behind the enemy's lines by parachute.

PART 2

THE SOE AGENTS
BORN IN BRIGHTON

Chapter 4

LIEUTENANT JACQUELINE NEARNE
MBE CROIX DE GUERRE
FRENCH SECTION

Jacqueline Nearne in her FANY uniform.
Photo: author's coll.

THE LATE PROFESSOR MICHAEL FOOT, AUTHOR OF THE BRITISH GOVERN-
ment's first official history of the Special Operations Executive – '*SOE in France*' - quoted
the Roman philosopher Boethius who, in the 6th century, observed:

"Splendid men often go unnoticed because there is no one to tell their tale".

In the case of SOE, it was very much the case, as evidenced by the following account,
that splendid women served alongside these splendid men. One of SOE's recruiting officers, Captain Selwyn Jepson, explained, in an interview recorded long after the war, how
the service first started to recruit women for service in the field:

'I was responsible for recruiting women for the work, in the face of a good deal of
opposition, I may say, from the powers that be. In my view, women were very much
better than men for the work. Women, as you must know, have a far greater capacity
for cool and lonely courage than men. Men usually want a mate with them. Men
don't work alone; their lives tend to be always in company with other men. There was
opposition from most quarters until it went up to Churchill, whom I had met before
the war. He growled at me, "What are you doing?" I told him and he said, "I see you
are using women to do this" and I said, "Yes, don't you think it is a very sensible thing
to do?" and he said, "Yes, good luck to you". That was my authority!'

One of the women recruited by Jepson who was to prove him right was Jacqueline
Françoise Mary Josephine Nearne. In 1913, in London, her father John 'Jack' Nearne had
married Mariquita Carmen de Piazaola, the aristocratic daughter of a Spanish Count and a
French Marquise. The couple's first child, Francis, was born in 1914, by which time the family
home was at 32 West Hill Street in Brighton. It was here that Jacqueline was born on 27 May
1916 while her father, who had been a medical student, served in the First World War in the
Royal Army Medical Corps. At the end of the war, Jack Nearne returned to civilian life as a
dispensing chemist and relocated the family back to London. In the new home in Fulham
the family continued to grow with the addition of another son, Frederick, in 1920 and finally
with a second daughter, Eileen (known as 'Didi') in 1921. In 1923 the Nearnes left England
and with the help of Mariquita's wealthy family, settled in an apartment in Paris. Jacqueline
attended the private Catholic Convent School of Les Oiseaux at Verneuil. After only two
years, however, the family moved again when Mariquita's parents gave them a seafront house
in Boulogne-sur-Mer. Jacqueline and Didi attended the town's Ursuline convent and both
became completely bi-lingual. Jacqueline was an active girl, enjoying cycling and playing in a
local hockey team. She made many friends, including a young British boy, Brian Stonehouse,
whose family had moved from England to Wimereux, only five kilometres along the coast
from Boulogne. Stonehouse and Jacqueline were to renew their friendship during and after
the Second World War.

The Nearne family were happy in their Boulogne home, but a further opportunity occurred
after the death of Mariquita's mother who bequeathed her daughter a more substantial house

Jacqueline was born at 32 West Hill Street, Brighton. Photo: Malcolm, Conor and Lucas Hatch.

in the old town of Nice, on the Côte d'Azur. The appeal of the setting and the better climate led to another relocation in 1931 and when Jacqueline finished her schooling at the age of 18, she became a sales representative for a Nice-based office equipment company. Her work entailed travel throughout France, experience that would later serve her well during her war service.

When war broke out in 1939, the Nearne household was initially largely unaffected, but all changed with the capitulation of France in June 1940. Foreign subjects were forced to move from the coastal areas of France and this doubly applied to the Nearnes who found they would not be allowed to live in either Nice or their previous home in Boulogne, which they had closed up, but not sold. The Nice property was therefore rented out and Jack, Mariquita, Jacqueline, Frederick and Didi found themselves again on the move, finding a property in Saint-Egrève, near to Grenoble in the unoccupied zone of France and close to where the eldest son, Francis, was then living after marrying a Frenchwoman. This latest move prompted Frederick to leave for England in the autumn of 1940, determined to join the RAF.

In the wake of her brother's departure to serve Britain, Jacqueline's own determination grew to help the country of her birth and Didi became infused with the same spirit. They contacted the British Consulate that still operated in Vichy France in Lyons, obtained British passports and in early 1942 left their parents' home for Marseilles, from where they hoped to take a ship to neutral Spain or Portugal, from where they could continue to Britain.

Their first attempt ended in failure when they were refused sea passage and ordered to return to Grenoble. A second effort, in April, saw them succeed in travelling by train via Spain to Portugal. From there they were unable to travel directly to Britain, but the British Consulate in Lisbon arranged to put them aboard a merchant ship bound for Gibraltar. After only three days on the Rock they boarded another ship and at last reached Britain when they docked in the River Clyde in Scotland several days later. Jacqueline and her sister initially stayed with family friends in north London while they investigated how they might serve Britain. Jacqueline was disappointed when her application to join the Women's Royal Naval Service (WRNS) as a driver was turned down, but shortly afterwards she received a letter from Captain Selwyn Jepson inviting her to interview at the War Office in Horseguards in London.

Jepson interviewed Jacqueline on 25 June 1942 and soon cut to the direct question as to whether she might consider returning to France in a clandestine role. The proposition took Jacqueline by surprise as she had been anticipating work as a translator or interpreter, but Jepson urged her to think it over after the interview while he considered whether she might be suitable.

Only a few days later Jepson wrote to confirm that he did feel Jacqueline was capable of the work at which he had hinted. She accepted and by 9 July 1942 Jepson's was one of two letters of recommendation for Jacqueline to be taken on charge by the First Aid Nursing Yeomanry (FANY) whose Women's Transport Service (WTS) headquarters were also in Horseguards. The use of the FANY resulted from the fact the service was not officially part of the British armed forces, though the FANY operated in a variety of support roles for the military. This therefore sidestepped the policy that women in the armed forces should not serve in the front line or in combat, while at the same time it gave women agents some form of rank which, it was hoped, might guarantee them better treatment in the event of capture and imprisonment. The fact that membership of the FANY was no more than a cover story was underlined by Jepson, in his letter of recommendation penned only days after meeting Jacqueline, but stating 'I have known this applicant socially, for a considerable period.........'.

The training of women agents for service in the field was still a new matter for French Section and in these early days it was felt that the women trainees did not require the same syllabus as the men. Consequently, Jacqueline joined a first small group of women, Party 27 0B, which received neither the usual preliminary training at STS 5 at Wanborough Manor in Surrey, nor a paramilitary training course in Scotland. Instead, the group only underwent the parachute course at STS 51, RAF Ringway and a Finishing School course at STS 31, which consisted of two country houses, 'The Rings' and (STS 31a) 'The House in the Wood', at Beaulieu. While she did not enjoy the parachute training, Jacqueline nevertheless passed the course, but at Beaulieu she found herself the subject of a less-than-glowing report. In his assessment of her, the commandant of STS 31, Lieutenant-Colonel Woolrych, found Jacqueline to be reserved, shy and a 'very simple person'. And although he noted 'a certain amount of determination' he concluded: 'she might very well develop after long and careful training, but at present she could not be recommended'.

STS 31 The Rings (left) and STS 31a The House in the Wood at Beaulieu. Photo: author's coll.

Despite this negative report, Jacqueline was cleared for operational service when Major Buckmaster, head of French Section, annotated her file with his personal view that Jacqueline was 'one of the best we have had'. Given that Buckmaster would have known only a little more than Jepson about Jacqueline, when Jepson had written to the FANY with his supposed knowledge of her 'for a considerable period', this was a dramatic gesture of faith. Buckmaster was to provide similar over-riding comments in respect of a number of other women trainees, and was largely proved justified in the light of their subsequent performance in the field.

Captain Selwyn Jepson (left) and Major Maurice Buckmaster, head of F Section, both identified Jacqueline's ability and commitment, in contrast to Beaulieu's negative report on her. Photo: author's coll.

With Buckmaster's backing, Jacqueline was approved to work as a courier in France and was introduced to the man who would be her circuit leader, Flight Lieutenant (later Squadron Leader) Maurice Southgate (STATIONER/*Hector*). Jacqueline's own code name was to be DESIGNER, her field name was her own name, *Jacqueline*, and her false identity in France was in the name of Josette Norville, with a cover story of being a sales representative of a Lyons-based pharmaceutical company. Thanks to her background in a not-dissimilar job, Jacqueline was expected to have little difficulty in adapting to the role and also to the long train journeys that would be involved. This extensive travelling was necessary since STATIONER was to cover an almost impossibly large area, stretching some 550 kilometres from Châteauroux (36), in the Indre *département* of central France, to Tarbes (65) in the Hautes-Pyrénées *département* in the south-west of the country.

Orders for the despatch of Southgate and Jacqueline were first issued in late October 1942, but the first attempt, from RAF Tempsford in Bedfordshire, was aborted when the pilot of their Halifax aircraft received no signal from the arranged reception committee on the ground in France. Three more attempts failed, due to either poor weather conditions or technical fault and it was not until 25 January 1943 that the pair were dropped 'blind' i.e. without a reception committee to welcome them, by Flight Lieutenant Prior from a Halifax of 161 (Special Duties) Squadron from RAF Tempsford. They landed, without incident, on the targeted DZ (drop zone) near Espalem (43) in the Haute-Loire *département*. After gathering their bags, they set off to find the station in Brioude, some 14 kilometres away, from where they would take a train to the safe house of the Néraud family in Clermont-Ferrand. But as they walked along a country lane at first light, still not entirely sure that they were heading in the right direction, an incident occurred which was to gain a place in SOE folklore. Seeing a woman approaching on a bicycle, Southgate hailed her and queried the way to the station – in English. The startled look on the woman's face only disappeared when Jacqueline quickly repeated the question in French and the moment of danger passed.

Jacqueline parachuted into France from a Halifax aircraft of 161 (Special Duties) Squadron, based at RAF Tempsford. Photo: author's coll.

The rest of the journey, once the station at Brioude was reached, went smoothly and at the Nérauds' house they made contact with George Jones (LIME/*Isidore*) who was the W/T operator to the circuit of Brian Rafferty (AUBRETIA/*Dominique*). Until the arrival of Southgate's own W/T operator, Jones would transmit messages for Southgate, with Jacqueline acting as courier between them.

For the first few weeks, Jacqueline supported Southgate in establishing contact with *Résistance* groups throughout the large area in which the STATIONER circuit was expected to operate. For Jacqueline, whose primary role was to carry messages to and from the *Résistance* cells, this meant long and tiring journeys by crowded and frequently–delayed trains, with the result that she was often sleep-deprived. From April, STATIONER received its own W/T operator in the form of Lieutenant (later Major) Amédée Maingard (SHIPWRIGHT/ *Samuel*), for whom Jacqueline was responsible for finding lodgings in the rue de la Gare in Châteauroux. Once settled there, Maingard became the hub of all communications for the circuit, with Jacqueline visiting him several times a week to collect or deliver messages. Though frequently staying in hotels, Jacqueline's main base remained with the ever-supportive Néraud family in Clermont-Ferrand. From there she was also able to visit her brother, Francis, who had remained living with his wife and son outside Grenoble. Once he learned of his sister's work, Francis agreed to help Jacqueline in courier work for the STATIONER circuit, but was fortunate not to be arrested when, in September 1943, the Germans raided the Nérauds' house in the rue Blatin while Francis was staying there. Monsieur and Madame Néraud and their teenage daughter, Colette, were arrested, but Francis avoided capture and Jacqueline, who had been due to return to the house the same evening, was warned of the disaster and kept her distance.

As a consequence of his narrow escape, Francis became anxious for himself and his family, yet at the same time resolved he should do more for the war effort and

Jacqueline's circuit leader in STATIONER was Flight Lieutenant Maurice Southgate (left - in both RAF uniform and, inset, in civilian clothing for his French false ID).

The network's W/T operator was Lieutenant Amédée Maingard. Photos: Maingard coll.

Eileen 'Didi' Nearne, sister to Jacqueline, also joined F Section and served with distinction. Photo: author's coll.

emulate his two sisters in going to England. In October, Jacqueline therefore made arrangements, with Southgate's approval and via Maingard's W/T set, for Francis to be flown out of France, with a view to being trained and returned as a French Section agent. Francis arrived in Britain just as his youngest sister Didi (who had followed Jacqueline into French Section) was completing her own training as a W/T operator. Francis, however, was to prove unsuitable as a trainee and did not return to France.

Another traveller to Britain in October 1943 was Southgate, recalled in order to report on his activities to date and to be briefed for STATIONER'S role in support of the long-awaited invasion of France. But bad winter weather meant his return to France was delayed until January 1944 and in his absence, Jacqueline, Amédée Maingard and their local helpers had much to do. An additional woman agent courier, Pearl Witherington (WRESTLER/ *Mariè*) had arrived in late September 1943 to help lighten the load when Southgate had become concerned that Jacqueline was becoming exhausted. The two women did not work together, but Pearl was later to recall that she was told Jacqueline had become so weak that she could not carry a case with her on her journeys. Upon hearing of her exhaustion while he was still in England, Southgate recommended her recall in January 1944, but although the order for her return was sent via Maingard, Jacqueline refused to obey it, believing that she could not be spared at a critical time. For in addition to Southgate's continuing absence, Maingard was showing dissatisfaction with his role and confessed to 'having the blues'. Jacqueline was one of the few contacts he had and though she tried to buoy up his spirits, Maingard longed for more action and contemplated asking London to recall him so that he might become a commando. To add to the challenges, Auguste Chantraine, the locally-recruited leader of STATIONER's most northerly group in and around Châteauroux, had been arrested just before Christmas and then Pearl had fallen ill with a bout of neuralgic rheumatism. So, though Buckmaster at SOE headquarters continued to press for Jacqueline's return, she preferred to soldier on to the best of her ability. After Southgate's return to France, this included helping in the acclimatisation to everyday French life of a young French-Canadian W/T operator, Lieutenant Allyre Sirois (SATYR/*Gustave*) who had been dropped on the night of 1/2 March 1944 to a STATIONER reception. Sirois' accent, and his ignorance of French customs and life, startled those who received him - to the extent that they immediately hid him away in a safe house in Toulouse where Jacqueline visited him to contribute to his French 'schooling'. Otherwise, it was only a matter of time before Jacqueline was compelled to return to England and she was taken in by another element of STATIONER's *résistance familiale*, Monsieur and Madame Bidet in Montluçon (03), who did their best to ensure Jacqueline rested and recovered.

When, as expected, the recall order was again received from England, Jacqueline reluctantly agreed, on condition that she should later be allowed to return to France to continue serving in the field once her health was sufficiently robust. For her extraction, STATIONER's air operations expert, Lieutenant Alexandre Schwatschko (POLITICIAN/*Olive*), had identified a landing ground, codenamed BILLIARD, two kilometres south south-west of Villers-les-Orme (36) and eight kilometres north-west of Châteauroux. Jacqueline stayed at a farm close to the field, sharing the wait with Jean Savy (WIZARD/*Régis*) who needed to return to England with vital information regarding the enemy's V-weapons. Though Jacqueline did not yet know it, Savy was the circuit leader of her sister Didi, now serving the WIZARD *réseau* in Paris as a W/T operator with the codename PIONEER and field name *Rose*. At last the message was received to expect the aircraft on the night of 9/10 April 1944, but shortly before it arrived, a third passenger arrived in the form of Josette, wife of Southgate. Given that the aircraft was only a small Lysander, three people in addition to the pilot was the maximum payload and the incoming flight brought the same number of agents, including Lise de Baissac, Jacqueline's friend from her training days. As the Lysander taxied to a halt, a chalked message could be seen on the black fuselage, scrawled there by Buckmaster who had been at RAF Tangmere to see the aircraft off. Leaving nothing to chance, it read:

> Batting order:
> 1. Jacqueline
> 2. If possible Josette.
> This is an order.

Buckmaster had clearly not known the importance of the intelligence that Savy was bringing to England.

The return flight, of what was termed OPERATION CHAUFFEUR, passed without incident until Flight Lieutenant Taylor approached the English south coast. There, he found that 161 Squadron's forward operating base of RAF Tangmere was fogged in and despite being low on fuel, Taylor was obliged to continue inland. Fortunately, after some 30 miles, he found RAF Dunsfold, near Godalming in Surrey, was clear and made a safe landing.

Jacqueline returned to England in a Lysander of 161 Squadron. Photo: author's coll.

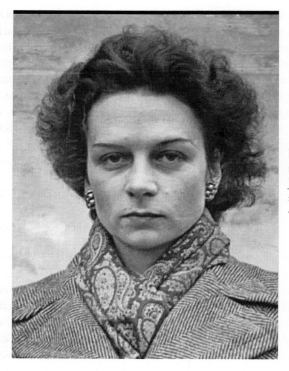

Fatigue from her time in France shows clearly in this photograph of Jacqueline after her return. Photo: author's coll.

Taken by car up to SOE headquarters in Baker Street, Jacqueline could at last unwind after 15 months of tension in the field. She found herself promoted to Lieutenant and warmly welcomed back by Buckmaster, whose decision to overturn her training school's rejection had been amply vindicated. After a full debriefing regarding her activities in France, Jacqueline enjoyed two months' of recuperation until she declared herself ready to return to active duty. It was initially decided, however, that she would first benefit from refresher training and then instruction in other operational responsibilities such as use of the ground-to-air S-phone, the Eureka transmitting beacon and the art of organising reception committees for landings and drops from aircraft. Her refresher course was at STS 42 at Roughwood Park, Chalfont St Giles in Buckinghamshire where she was summarised as:

'A very pleasant student who worked hard at all times and has made very considerable progress......During her stay here she regained a great deal of her physical and nervous strength'.

The latter comment reflected the fact that Jacqueline spent at least a month at STS 42 before, in mid-July, she progressed to additional operational training at STS 40, Howbury Hall, near Waterend, Great Barford, in Bedfordshire. In nine days of tuition that finished in mid-July, she was again judged to have worked well and was described as keen and hardworking. But

Publicity and stills from the film 'School for Danger' in which Jacqueline starred. Photos: Martyn Cox; Imperial War Museum - FLM 1244; FLM 1250

her satisfaction at passing the course was destroyed a week later when news reached French Section that her sister Didi had been arrested in France. This latest bad news added to the fact that Southgate had been arrested back in May and SOE headquarters had already agreed that Amédée Maingard and Pearl Witherington would divide the STATIONER circuit responsibilities between them by creating two separate networks – SHIPWRIGHT operated by Maingard and WRESTLER, led by Pearl. Neither had a role for Jacqueline and as the Allied armies continued their advance through France, time was fast running out for her to return to the field. Buckmaster consequently selected Jacqueline to play the lead role in a film of French Section's activities, commissioned by the British government's Central Office of Information. Though Jacqueline's character was fictitious, the film accurately portrayed elements of SOE's syllabus for agents, including paramilitary and W/T training, and the operation of the Special Duties squadrons. Completed in 1944, but not released until 1946 under the title 'Now It Can Be Told', the film was later shortened for the cinema and renamed 'School For Danger'. It is still commercially available today.

A last duty for SOE saw Jacqueline accompanying several other agents and Baker Street headquarters staff on one of Colonel Buckmaster's 'Judex' missions that toured F Section's former operational areas in France in October and November of 1944. Designed to help thank the local people who had assisted SOE agents, as well as to hopefully gain more information on the activities of agents such as Didi Nearne who had subsequently been captured and disappeared, the Judex tour which Jacqueline joined led to Buckmaster noting:

'I shall never forget the warmth of the family embraces which were showered on Jacqueline….they bore testimony to her popularity and to her unselfishness'.

In respect of the still-missing Didi, nothing more was learned by Jacqueline until, in May 1945, the news reached London that Didi had managed to survive her imprisonment in Germany and would be returning. Her health was poor from her experience and Jacqueline therefore spent the next few months helping Didi regain her strength, while also looking for gainful employment. This came in November 1945 when Jacqueline began work in London as a secretary for the newly-created United Nations Organisation (UN). When it was subsequently decided that the UN would be based in New York, Jacqueline agreed to transfer there and sailed for the United States in April 1946. She soon progressed from secretarial work and built a career as a liaison officer, looking after the New York-based representatives of member nations. She had extended leave every two years which enabled her to return to England to see Didi and during her first return trip Jacqueline also travelled to France in order to receive honorary citizenship from Boulogne-sur-Mer where she had lived as a child. Brian Stonehouse, her childhood acquaintance from Boulogne who had also become an SOE agentwith French Section, was working in Washington and New York as an illustrator for the Elizabeth Arden company and for Vogue and Harper's Bazaar magazines. The two resumed their friendship and Stonehouse painted the striking portrait of Jacqueline (entitled 'The Cat', after her role in 'Now It Can Be Told') that now hangs in the Special Forces Club in London.

Brian Stonehouse, childhood friend in France and fellow-agent in F Section, survived capture and concentration camp to renew his friendship with Jacqueline in post-war New York and London. Photo: Sharf coll.

While Stonehouse was one of many dedicated friends in the United States, no one was close enough to warrant Jacqueline remaining there when she retired from the UN in 1978, after 32 years' service. She settled in an apartment in Belgravia in London, but only four years later became seriously ill with cancer. Didi moved in to help care for her, but on 15 August 1982 Jacqueline died, aged only 66 years.

Sources and acknowledgements: I first became aware of Jacqueline when writing the biography of the STATIONER network's W/T operator, Amédée Maingard DSO. Since then her biography, together with that of her sister, Didi, has been written by Susan Ottaway who has generously allowed me to use material from '*Sisters, Secrets and Sacrifice*', Harper, 2013, ISBN 978-0-00-749305-0. For further reading on Jacqueline's life, this book is strongly recommended.

Jacqueline's SOE personal file is in the UK National Archives (TNA), ref. HS9/1089/4 and she features in the files of Southgate HS9/1395/3 and Maingard HS9/976/9.

CHAPTER 5

CAPTAIN RONALD TAYLOR ITALIAN SECTION (NO. 1 SPECIAL FORCE)

Photo : Dr Rod Taylor

MANY WRITERS ABOUT SOE, INCLUDING MYSELF, HAVE TENDED TO concentrate on operations in support of French resistance. France was the largest and most-important occupied country in Western Europe and as it was to become the target of the allied invasion of northern Europe, it was natural that the Allies should devote most of their attention to supporting the resistance forces there. The exploits of SOE agents in France, particularly of the women agents, have consequently attracted most literary and film attention and the first official history of SOE, published on behalf of the British government in 1966, was Professor Michael Foot's invaluable 'SOE in France'.

But the operations of SOE in other countries and theatres have more recently begun to attract attention, particularly so since the SOE archives were released to The National Archives at Kew. Many of the stories from other theatres rival those from France in terms of heroism, tragedy and achievement. One major example of success was the sabotage of the Norwegian heavy-water plant which disrupted and crucially delayed the German atomic research programme. At the other end of the spectrum was the *Englandspiel* successfully played by the German military intelligence service, the *Abwehr*, that led so many Dutch SOE agents to their deaths. But most of SOE's operations in all theatres were more tactical and less spectacular, involving sabotage of factories, power supplies, means of transportation and supply (including roads, bridges, railways, vehicles, ships and aircraft) and supplying, training and coordinating the operations and supply of resistance groups which carried out operations in occupied countries.

One such theatre of war that has not received the same attention as France, is Italy. Captain Ron Taylor, Brighton-born, raised and educated, was an SOE officer who went through a very different training programme to that of French Section personnel. His role was not that of a secret agent, working clandestinely, but as a specialist military support officer, in uniform, dropped behind the enemy's lines to operate alongside resistance and partisan forces. He was nominally listed as being in the Italian Section of SOE, but in practice came under the command of SOE's No. 1 Special Force where he served with success and distinction.

Ronald Gordon Taylor, known as Ron, was born on 2 October 1916, the youngest of the ten children (only eight survived infancy) of Thomas Samuel Taylor and Jane Taylor (née Luckhurst). While his father had been born in Lancashire of Cheshire stock, his mother was born in Brighton and the family was living at 29 Carlton Street, Brighton, when Ron was born. In between her frequent periods of child birth, Jane worked as a charlady at the Brighton Pavilion. Her husband, Thomas, worked as a swimming instructor, but soon after Ron's birth, he was conscripted into the British Army in 1917 during the First World War, despite his relatively-advanced age of 42. He served on the Western Front in the 305th Road Construction Company of the Royal Engineers and was fortunate to miss the terrible Battle of Paschendaele, having been knocked down by a motor-cycle dispatch rider and invalided home.

Ron attended his local elementary school, St John's, in Carlton Hill, Brighton until 1928, Varndean Secondary School in the town until 1935, and then undertook an external University of London BSc (Eng) degree at Brighton Municipal Technical College, graduating in 1937. He joined AE Watson as a draughtsman and designer of steel structures. By

Carlton Street, Brighton – demolished in 1937 as part of a slum clearance project by Brighton Council. Photo: City of Brighton and Hove.

this time the family was living at 5 Mount Pleasant in Brighton, but Ron moved to London in connection with his work and it was there that, only weeks after the outbreak of war, he joined the British Army on 18 October 1939.

Above left: the former Brighton Municipal Technical College in Richmond Terrace, Brighton, now private apartments. Photo – author. Above right: 5 Mount Pleasant to where the family moved after the demolition of 29 Carlton Street. Photo: Dr Rod Taylor.

Following his father's example in the First World War, Taylor joined the Royal Engineers, He served as a Sapper (Private) with the service number 2192989 in the Depot Company of the 1st Training Battalion, Royal Engineers (No 1 TBRE) at Shorncliffe Camp in Kent where duties were enlivened by the garrison being responsible for defence of the coastal sector Hythe-Folkestone in the event of what was then a very much expected German invasion. In October 1940 he was accepted as an officer cadet and posted to 141 Officer Cadet Training Unit (OCTU) of the Royal Engineers, also at Shorncliffe. He passed out from the course in March 1941, was commissioned at Aldershot as a Second Lieutenant with the new service number 179725 and was quickly promoted to full Lieutenant the following month. He then spent two years, from March 1941 to July 1943, as an officer at the British Army's Experimental Bridging Establishment at Christchurch, becoming an expert on military bridging and helping design the original Bailey Bridge.

Taylor, centre, with two other new recruits at Shorncliffe Camp in May 1940. Photo: Taylor coll.

A prototype Bailey Bridge, worked on by Taylor, can still be seen over Ma Siller's channel, Stanpit Marsh, Christchurch. Photo: author.

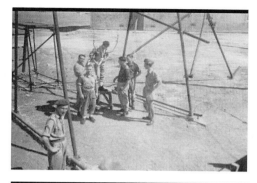

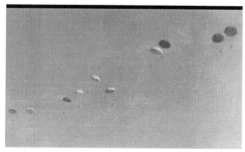

Parachute training at Ramat David in Palestine (now Israel). Photos: Taylor coll.

Taylor continued to develop his professional status as a Structural Engineer and Chartered Engineer, but though he was posted to 510 Royal Engineer Field Company from July 1943, he sought a more active role in the war by volunteering for SOE in October of the same year. He was security-cleared within the month in London by MI5, allocated the SOE service number 15785, and signed the Official Secrets Act on 8 November 1943.

SOE's plans for Taylor centred on using his technical expertise in support of sabotage operations by partisans in southern Europe and the Balkans. He would first need further specialised training, but unlike that provided in England for personnel destined for western or northern Europe, he was posted to SOE's MO4 branch, at GHQ Middle East Forces in Cairo. He left the UK by air on 24 November 1943, was formally taken on charge by MO4 on 28 November and reported in Cairo on 30 November for posting to Force 133, the unit responsible for SOE's operations with partisan and resistance forces in northern Italy and the Balkans. In order to join Force 133, Taylor required parachute and paramilitary training. For the former, in December 1943 he attended a course at the RAF airfield at Ramat David, 30 kilometres south-east of Haifa in what was then Palestine, now Israel, where trainees learned to jump from Douglas C-47 (Dakota) and Hudson aircraft.

It was then not until May 1944 that Taylor completed a paramilitary course at Special Training School 102 (STS 102 – also known as Military Establishment/ME 102), housed in the abandoned Stella Maris monastery on the westernmost slope of Mount Carmel, above the town of Haifa and overlooking the Mediterranean Sea. His course there, number 13, consisted of map reading, fieldcraft, demolitions, weapon training, physical exercise and Morse code. It included a 10-day hike into Lebanon and Syria before returning to Haifa; a mule-handling course; and ski training at a British Army 'Snow School' in the Lebanese mountains.

Left: STS 102, SOE's training school at Haifa in Palestine, was sited in the vacated Stella Maris monastery on Mount Carmel. Photo - Karimeh Abbud.

Left and above - The syllabus at STS 102 included handling mules, learning to ski in mountain warfare conditions and befriending the local population. Photos: Taylor coll.

Taylor was rated 'good' or 'very good' throughout this training, albeit with the sobering added comment 'requires further practice in Silent Killing'. He received a category B rating overall and his Chief Instructor's comments on 15 May 1944 read:

'The best student of the course in every respect. Very keen and conscientious and reached a good standard in all subjects. Particularly good in demolitions. Should prove an extremely useful operative'.

The commandant of STS 102 added:

'A hard-working officer who, starting with the initial advantage of being a Sapper, took the course seriously, learnt a lot and produced good results. Technically competent, he is intelligent and has good "soldiering sense". He has a mind of his own and is not afraid to criticise. Not the type to "suffer fools gladly" – given a job to do which requires common sense, attention to detail, technical ability and guts he should do it very well'.

Having passed with flying colours, Taylor was posted to SOE's forward headquarters in Italy, joining No. 1 Special Force at Monopoli, 45 kilometres south-east along the coast from Bari. There, Taylor was briefed as one of a three-man team to be sent to the already-operational COOLANT mission of Major Hedley Vincent. The latter had been the first British Liaison Officer (BLO) to be dropped to assist Italian partisan units after the liberation of Rome. Together with two W/T operators, Sergeant Macdonnell and Sergeant Hargreaves, Vincent had parachuted into the Friuli region of north-east Italy in June 1944 to instruct and support the Italian partisan forces who were rapidly organising and expanding in strength against the German forces still tenaciously occupying the area. The original drop of Vincent and Macdonnell had been codenamed SERMON and the operation to parachute Taylor and his colleagues was therefore named SERMON II. Taylor and his fellow-officer, Lieutenant David Godwin of the Royal Armoured Corps, were to add their specialist skills in sabotage and the use of explosives and they were accompanied, as interpreter, by Corporal Michael "Micky" Trent, formerly of the Royal Army Service Corps and No 2 Commando, recruited by SOE in Palestine. Trent's real name was Issack Michael Gyori, a Czech-born Hungarian Jew who could speak twelve different languages reasonably fluently and would be much-needed since neither Taylor nor Godwin spoke Italian. Though he had learned basic French and German at school, Taylor had absolutely no knowledge of the Italian language, but Godwin was to find he could generate a limited amount of understanding thanks to his being fluent in Spanish.

The operation took place on the night of 12/13 August 1944 and was undertaken by an unarmed Dakota to the drop zone (DZ) that had been established by Major Vincent, known locally by the pseudonym "Major Tucker". The DZ, codenamed BEAVERTON, was just to the north of the village of Canebola, in meadow land near the hamlet of Porzûs and on the upper slopes of Monte Joanez, close to the summit. The bonfires marking the DZ were shielded to some extent by the mountainous terrain, but the weather was so fine and clear that the fires' glow could be seen for miles around in the area, fortunately without any enemy response. All three men jumped without incident and landed within a few metres of the fires, Taylor being enthusiastically welcomed by an Italian partisan who kissed him vigorously on both cheeks.

The BEAVERTON drop zone was located some 300 metres to the north of the village of Canebola, on the upper slopes of Monte Joanez. Photo – author's collection.

As soon as there was available dawn light, the new arrivals (together with the supplies of weapons, ammunition and explosives that had been dropped with them) were taken by their reception party to Canebola where, accompanied by Major Vincent, they aroused great and welcoming interest. The team's principal task was to train the partisans in the use of explosives for sabotage and to ensure that operations against the enemy were part of a planned and co-ordinated programme. Training courses, each lasting three to four days, were held either in the open, weather permitting, or in schools – in Canebola itself and at various villages throughout the area including Stremiz, Porzûs and Robedischis (later Robidišče, after post-war border changes placed the community a few hundred metres inside Yugoslavia, now Slovenia).

Priority targets for COOLANT and their partisan groups were the road and railway running from Venice up to Austria through the Pontebba pass, along which the enemy were carrying vital supplies to the front and, in the opposite direction, a considerable quantity of war booty. The railway line in particular had been subject to heavy, but unsuccessful, bombing by the USAAF, but the partisans fared much better after Taylor and Godwin's instruction. They were trained to take only a few seconds to place explosive charges on the line, in darkness, and to also plant more charges, with time pencils, in the surrounding area so that repair efforts in the following days would be disrupted. The frequency and success of sabotage on this line was extensive, leading the enemy to attempt (without success) to patrol it constantly, between strongpoints, in the area around Reana del Rojale. A secondary target was the road leading into Austria from the Yugoslavian side of the border, which passed through the old battle ground of Caporetto where the Italians had been defeated at the hands of the Austrians and Germans in the First World War. As and when targets of opportunity presented themselves, headquarters were alerted via Sergeant Macdonnell's W/T set and Allied fighter-bombers were dispatched if the weather permitted.

Taylor's colleagues in the second element of the COOLANT mission were (left) Corporal Issack Gyori (aka Micky Trent) and Lieutenant David Godwin. Photos: Taylor coll.

Resistance efforts were hampered, however by the tensions among the different partisan groups with which COOLANT had to work. The Garibaldi Natisone Brigade, with which Vincent had first made contact, was a left-wing and communist group of 500 or so and was distinguished by the wearing of red scarves. But after Vincent had established a good working relationship with, and had begun arranging air drops of weapons and supplies for, this unit, he then established links with a Republican partisan organisation, the Osoppo Brigade. Sporting green scarves, the Osoppo were firmly anti-communist and consequently viewed the *Garibaldini* with mistrust. In return, the *Garibaldini* were deeply suspicious of the Osoppo who had many former officers of the Italian Army among their ranks and who were therefore considered fascists. Vincent only managed to get the two brigades working together, as the *Divisione Garibaldi Osoppo* and with an eventual strength of around 2000 men and women, by threatening the withdrawal of all air drops, but he used Taylor, Godwin and Gyori to especially liaise with the Osoppo group. They immediately set about training small groups of selected partisans in sabotage and the use of explosives and to make an early positive impression on both the partisans and headquarters back in Monopoli, several kilometres of high-tension electricity pylons were destroyed in the first week. By chance, this proved to be a vital link in the supply for the whole of the Friuli region and thereby plunged a wide area into darkness. Its effect on the local population, as opposed to that on the enemy, was mitigated by the fact that many smaller villages did not have any electricity supply. The newly-trained partisan sabotage specialists, identifiable by a uniform badge that Taylor had devised for those who had passed his and Godwin's courses, went on to derail a train shortly afterwards. The Nobel 808 plastic explosive that they used, supplied by SOE, led the Italians to give Taylor and Godwin a *nome di battagli* and they consequently became known as, respectively, "*Tenente* [Lieutenant] *Plastico*" and "*Tenente 808*". Major Vincent was later to describe approvingly the infectious enthusiasm of his two Lieutenants: 'Taylor and Godwin were dead keen on explosives. They did things that you read about in *Rover* and *Wizard* [boys' comics of the time]. I can remember one time they got a damned big cheese, they were scooping out the middle of the cheese, and I said "What the hell are you doing there?". They said "We're going to put plastic in there. We'll put a time pencil in and get an Italian to take it down into the German mess in Udine".

Taylor's team of three principally supported Republican partisans. Photos: Taylor coll.

Over the two months following the arrival of Taylor, Godwin and Gyori, small groups of trained sabotage specialists, accompanied by increasingly better-armed partisans, attacked over forty supply trains. The same period saw the *missione inglese* and the partisans enjoying reasonable freedom of movement along their front line. The nearest enemy headquarters, at Faëdis, was evacuated in early August and the COOLANT mission moved its own base from Stremiz to Forame where, much to the enjoyment of the partisans, Taylor and the team implemented a daily ritual of raising and lowering the Union flag at the appropriate times of day. But as the British-supported offensive operations increased, so too did the enemy's response, often with brutal results. In a bizarre twist to the local conflict, between October 1944 and April 1945 about 38,000 Cossacks with their families, a total of 50,000 people, were transferred by train to the Friuli region which the Germans pledged would become *'Kosakenland in Nord Italien'*, the area having been assigned to them by the Commander of the German Army, Keitel, in exchange for the Cossacks' help in combatting the ever-mounting partisan guerrilla activity against the Third Reich. The Cossacks, together with other anti-communist ethnic groups of the USSR, had helped the Germans during their invasion of the Soviet Union, but as the tide of battle had turned against the Germans, the Cossacks had been obliged to follow the Nazis in their retreat and were assimilated into two divisions of the German Army. As reward for their help, they had been promised a settlement area elsewhere in Europe, other than in Germany. Consequently, when two areas of north-eastern Italy, namely Eastern Friuli (*'Friuli Orientale'*) which included Nimis, Attimis and Faedis; and the Friulian Alps (known as *'Carnia'*) had been proclaimed free zones by the partisan guerrillas earlier in 1944, four regiments of Cossacks were posted to Friuli to fight the partisans and to make the areas their own. Their arrival was an arresting spectacle. Some wore German uniforms, with Cossack variations and were well-armed, but many others still wore old Russian Tsarist cavalry uniforms, complete with huge busby-type hats, large ancient pistols, ammunition strapped over their chests, swords and daggers. Their horses were followed by caravans of wagons on which women, children and the elderly travelled with their cows, goats and even some camels. They lacked most basic supplies and would therefore frequently loot, pillage and steal from the local population who could ill-afford to lose the little they had. Opposition or protest usually met with killing and house burning by the Cossacks, who were in no mood to show leniency. One Cossack detachment, based in the village of Nimis, quickly became a nuisance to the Italian partisans' and the British Mission's road communications which had only recently been improved by the acquisition of a number of motorcycles. Taylor participated in the partisans' offensive which lasted some five days before a final assault on Nimis and surrender of the surviving Cossacks. No heavy weapons had been available, but automatic weapons had been dropped onto the BEAVERTON DZ and were augmented by a few Italian mortars and makeshift 'grenades' fashioned out of old cigarette tins filled with plastic explosives.

But the 'liberation' of Nimis was not to last long and COOLANT's stay in Forame came to a sudden end in early October. As the enemy's frustration had grown with the partisans' activities, the latter's intelligence network reported that the Germans were planning a strong 'round up' operation, a *rastrellamento*, using not only their local *Wehrmacht* units and the feared Cossacks, but also making use of crack *Jäger* mountain troops drafted in from

The village of Nimis was the scene of bitter fighting in late September 1944 between partisan forces and Cossacks serving in the German Army. Photos – author's collection.

Germany with armour and heavy weapons. The partisans deployed swiftly to defend the region in depth, roads and bridges were mined and roadblocks and ambush points created. One bridge on the vital railway was blown up as a south-bound train passed over it, cutting the train in half. The repair train and mobile crane that arrived the next day were similarly put out of action, but further action was then pre-empted by the launch of the enemy's attack which commenced at the end of September 1944 and reached Forame on the afternoon of 2 October 1944 when the village was almost surrounded by a strong enemy force. With ammunition running low, the partisans and their British advisers were forced to withdraw, covered by heavy rain which reduced visibility. Heading east and crossing the Natisone river, they marched for 36 hours in a non-stop deluge through dense forest that was so dark that each man had to hold onto the one in front to avoid becoming lost. Ten days later, Taylor and the team returned over the Natisone with a small nucleus of partisans and Sergeant Macdonnell was able to recover a hidden W/T battery. Within 30 seconds he had restored contact with Monopoli who had been anxiously waiting for news after contact was broken with COOLANT.

In early November 1944, Vincent was replaced by Captain (later Major) Tommy Macpherson, an experienced former commando who had fought in North Africa, escaped after being made a prisoner of war and had subsequently transferred to SOE where he had served in a Jedburgh team in France. Vincent returned to serve on the HQ staff of No 1 Special Force while the remainder of the COOLANT team remained to serve with Macpherson.

Captain Hedley Vincent (left) was replaced by Captain Tommy Macpherson in November 1944. Photos: Taylor coll.

Continuing enemy pressure meant, however, that the British and the partisans had to keep on the move. The rivers had turned into torrents that could only be crossed by bridges and the first snow had fallen. Orders transmitted from Monopoli included General Alexander's controversial instruction of 13 November 1944 to the partisans to cease large-scale operations against the enemy over the winter and to build up stocks of weapons and ammunition in anticipation of final efforts the following spring. Sabotage was therefore restricted to the occasional derailment of trains and the destruction of workshops that were making or repairing machines and parts for the Germans. One major act of sabotage that was still attempted was to destroy a fleet of locomotives, a substation, railway bridges and crossing points. Although meticulously planned and confirmed through special messages via the BBC, the attacks failed through poor communication at main British Army HQ and some 40 brave partisans were put at risk, several were captured and others died in the attempt. Taylor and the SERMON team were devastated and furious at the failure, but not once did any partisan apportion blame or hostility towards the team - a clear measure of the mutual respect between the British and the Italians. While offensive operations were reduced, intelligence gathering gained greater importance, especially since there was to be an Allied offensive in the spring. Details of strong points, troop movements, armaments, bridges and even, on one occasion, the type and thickness of concrete on a particular structure, were provided across a wide area. A town plan of Udine was produced, marking every known location of the enemy in what was to be a key objective of the coming attack.

The winter weather during this period was extremely harsh and Taylor and the other members of the team had nothing but their British Army standard issue uniform, complete with string vest which Taylor recalled had not been changed for months. Some of the partisans fared worse, without adequate clothing or footwear, but their commitment to the cause never wavered. New Year's Eve of 1944 was spent in a small cave, just two metres below the snow line on the saddle of a mountain overlooking Cividale. To the enjoyment of the partisans with them, the team insisted that the Italians join the British in a traditional rendering of *Auld Lang Syne*, cheering all concerned.

The close of 1944 and the advent of 1945 saw the Osoppo Division under orders to cross the border into Yugoslavia to join the IX Slovenian *Korpus* (Corps) of the Yugoslavian 2nd Army who were to lead in operations to help liberate the area on both sides of the Italo/Yugoslav border. Tensions were now even more pronounced, with the Yugoslavian partisans equally opposed to the Osoppo group and siding with the

Corporal Issack Gyori, pictured here on a mule at Stremis, was killed on Christmas Day, 1944 in disputed circumstances. Photo: Taylor coll.

pro-communist Garibaldi Natsione. Accusations of treachery and betrayal were rife and further exacerbated by Yugoslavian territorial designs on Trieste and the region to its north in which COOLANT was operating. A direct and tragic impact of this had come on Christmas Day 1944 when Corporal Issack Gyori Trent was reported killed by an enemy patrol when he had been sent on ahead by Macpherson, with an escort, to make contact with the Yugoslavian forces on the border. The circumstances of the tragedy are not clear and his body was not recovered, but Macpherson reported a claim that Trent was robbed and murdered by Slovenes, an accusation not subsequently proven by a later British investigation. Gyori's body was reported to have been buried in an unmarked grave, close to where he was killed while crossing the Isonzo [Soča] river near the village of Descla (now Deskle in Slovenia). He is commemorated as having no known grave on the Commonwealth War Graves Commission's Athens Memorial which covers most such deaths in the theatre.

COOLANT were now to accompany the Italian partisans ordered to join up with the Yugoslavs and on 12 January 1945 the team started on foot from Friuli, via the Osoppo partisan headquarters at the *malghe* (mountain huts) of Porzûs, towards the east. At the Osoppo command post, Taylor was fortunate to have a frozen foot treated by partisans who had served with the Italian mountain troops, the Alpini, in the invasion of Greece in 1940-41. After four weeks of arduous cross country trekking in snow-covered hilly and mountainous countryside, the partisan force and their British support mission reached Crnomolj in Yugoslavia and Taylor was brought out of the field by an RAF C-47 (Dakota) on 12 February 1945, returning to a promotion to the rank of Captain which had been processed in January after Lieutenant-Colonel Hewitt, commanding No. 1 Special Force, had written to headquarters saying of Taylor (and Godwin):

'These officers were infiltrated into the field some four months ago and have carried out their duties in a manner most praiseworthy under difficult conditions. Lieutenant Taylor is an outstanding worker, cheerful and competent, and inspires considerable confidence with all those with whom he comes in contact'.

And:

'this officer entered the Field in August 1944 as part of a British Mission under Major H. Vincent. In November 1944 Major Vincent found it necessary to establish two missions in the area in which he was operating. Lieutenant Taylor was given command of one of these Sub-missions w.e.f 3 November 1944 and has carried out the duties of a Mission leader since that date. Operating under most difficult conditions, this officer has proved himself to be fully competent and capable of carrying out these duties. As the leader of a Sub-mission he is responsible for organizing the activities of the partisan forces in the area under his command and for liaising with the heads of partisan forces in other areas......His promotion to Captain is most strongly recommended'.

Above - Taylor was brought out of
the field in a Dakota of the RAF, from
an airstrip in Yugoslavia. Both he and
Lieutenant Godwin (far right) were
promoted and awarded a Mention in
Despatches. Photos Taylor coll.

After his return, Taylor served from March 1945 on special operations air despatch duties
at the American (USAAF 12th Air Force) base at Rosignano airfield in north-western Italy
until, after the Axis surrender in Europe in May, his engineering expertise was put to good
use in public works when he was posted in June 1945 to work with the Allied Military
Government in Trieste. He served in that role until his release from the Army in 1946, at
which point he rejoined AE Watson as technical manager. He was awarded a Mention in
Despatches in March 1945 and the Italian Partisan Medal in July of the same year.

In 1947 Taylor was living and working in Exeter in Devon and in 1948 he joined
Costain John Brown Ltd. The same year saw him return to Brighton where he spent a short
period as a lecturer at his old college and spent some time living back at his parents' home
at 5 Mount Pleasant. In January 1949, he was appointed to a commission in the Intelligence
Corps as a Lieutenant, temporary Captain, in the Regular Army Reserve of Officers. This

Reserve appointment, not gazetted until August 1949, does not seem to have involved Taylor in any direct re-engagement in the Army and was not known to his (later) family.

He married (Ruby) Betty Harding, a girl he had met while working in Devon, in July 1949 and the following year saw the start of their family with the arrival of twin boys, Rod and John. Their home in 1951 was at 147 Carden Avenue and later, by 1956, at 46 York Avenue, Hove, by which time daughter Diane had arrived. Ron commuted to work in London from Hove until, in 1958, the family moved to Cheam in Surrey. Ron's engineering career meanwhile continued successfully, as a development engineer during a period with Tubewrights Ltd and then with Stewarts & Lloyds, later part of British Steel Tubes Division.

He played a leading role in developing and establishing structural engineering with tubes and hollow sections, notably the first Boeing 747 hangar for BOAC at Heathrow Airport, before leaving British Steel at the age of 59 and setting up his own practice as a consulting engineer. He was a member of the Council of the Institution of Structural Engineers, a Visiting Professor in the Department of Civil Engineering at Surrey University and a Master of the Worshipful Company of Constructors (1985/86) and continued to work into his eighties. His studies and experience provided him with the professional qualifications of BSc CEng FICE FIStructE FFB FWeldI. He returned to Italy on a number of occasions for post-war partisan reunions and events, being made an honorary Major in the Alpini Regiment. He appeared in a 1984 BBC television programme about SOE and participated in a 1987 conference of former SOE agents and partisans in Bologna, but otherwise spoke little of his wartime experiences. Having settled in later life in Buckinghamshire, in 2002 he moved to Dorchester, but only a few weeks later, died there on 10 December, aged 86.

Taylor and his family visited Italy on several occasions post-war and maintained contacts with veterans of the Osoppo partisan group. Photo: Taylor coll.

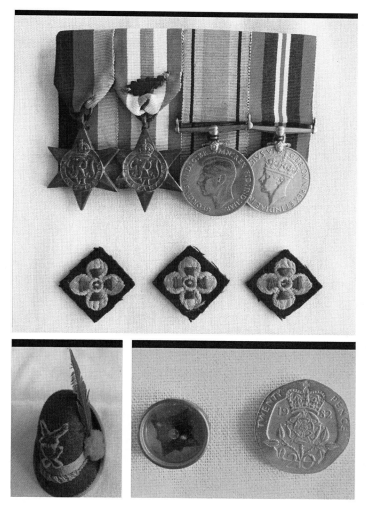

Memorabilia kept by Taylor's family includes his medals and Captain's rank badges; a miniature Alpini hat; and a compass that fitted into a button. Photos: Taylor coll.

Sources and acknowledgements: Ronald Taylor's SOE personal file is (TNA) HS9/1448/1 and COOLANT mission files are WO 06/3929; HS6/851/852/853 Italy - Political & Military Liaison Mission COOLANT - COOLANT BLUE V; HS9 640/6 is the personal file of Corporal Issack Gyori. Further information and memorabilia were kindly provided by Taylor's daughter, Diane Grainger and his son, Dr Rod Taylor. Published sources include: 'Mission Accomplished – SOE and Italy 1943-1945' by David Stafford; 'A Spur Called Courage – SOE Heroes in Italy' by Alan Ogden; 'Behind Enemy Lines' by Sir Tommy Macpherson with Richard Bath.

CHAPTER 6

CAPTAIN MICHAEL TROTOBAS
FRENCH SECTION

Photo: author's coll.

MICHAEL ALFRED RAYMOND TROTOBAS WAS BORN ON 20 MAY 1914, THE son of a French father, Henri, and mother Agnes (née Whelan) from Ireland. The two had met in Brighton where Henri Trotobas was a chef in the hotel industry. When the First World War broke out months later, Henri had returned to France to serve in the French Army, but had been captured the following year and spent three years as a prisoner of war. When he returned to Brighton to his wife and son, he resumed his work as a hotel chef, but his ill-treatment at the hands of his German captors later made a lasting impression on Michael.

The family home where Michael had been born was a small terraced house at 1 North Place in Brighton, originally built as married quarters for army personnel stationed at the local barracks, the rear windows of the house looking out onto what is still known as Barrack Yard. His childhood was one marked by physical endeavour, swimming in the sea and becoming a useful boxer, but when he was still only 9 years old tragedy struck with the death from TB of his mother, aged only 30, in 1923. For father Henri, the demand of a job with long and unsocial hours meant he could not cope with raising his son on his own. Neither could he afford help, so he was obliged to send Michael to live with his sister, Marie-Louise, back in the Var *département* of France from where Henri originated.

The birthplace of Trotobas at 1 North Place, Brighton. Photo: Martyn Cox.

Michael consequently spent two years at the Catholic school in St Cyr-sur-Mer, the French language posing no problems since his father had used it with him at home and had also arranged for Michael to have additional tutoring in the language from a friend among the French community in Brighton. For his secondary education, Michael attended another Catholic educational establishment, but this time in Dublin. Henri had arranged for Michael to live with Agnes's family while attending the Catholic University School of the Marist

Fathers with a view to Michael then progressing to the Catholic University. But after two fruitful years at the school, during which Michael became a fine all-round sportsman, he returned to France to complete his education at the Cours Fenelon, another Marist school, in Toulon. At the age of 16 he left school and returned to England where he became a cook, but after only four months he went back to France and worked in Paris, first as a sous-chef and then as an apprentice electrician. Eighteen months later and short of money, Michael was forced to return to his aunt in St Cyr-sur-Mer and spent several months there before again returning to England to see his father who had moved from Brighton to London. Taking a job as a factory worker and living in cheap rented accommodation near Victoria Station, Michael remained a restless spirit until, following a heart-to-heart talk with his father, he joined the regular British Army in April 1933.

Michael enlisted as an ordinary infantry soldier in the Middlesex Regiment (Duke of Cambridge's Own), nicknamed the 'Die Hards' after the exhortation of Lieutenant-Colonel William Inglis as he lay severely wounded at the Battle of Albuera in 1811. Refusing to be taken to the rear, he remained with the regimental colours and urged his men to hold their line against the French with the cry "Die hard, 57th, die hard!". Trotobas reported to the regimental depot named after this heroic officer, at Inglis Barracks, Mill Hill, London. Posted to the regiment's 2nd Battalion, he was quickly promoted to Lance-Corporal in the Battalion's B Company in 1934 and was based in Colchester barracks. His second stripe followed in 1936 and he continued to do well, honing his boxing skills as well as running the battalion's rugby team, a sport in which he excelled. In late 1936 the battalion moved to Portsmouth and then converted to become a machine gun battalion, moving to nearby Gosport in 1937. Michael took to his new duties with no difficulty, becoming an instructor on machine guns and all other infantry weapons.

Trotobas while serving in the Middlesex Regiment. Photo: author's coll.

In 1938 he was again promoted, to Lance Sergeant, and gained additional approbation by becoming the regiment's light-heavyweight boxing champion and a qualified lifeguard. When war was declared in September 1939 he was appointed as a Platoon Sergeant Major, a Warrant Officer rank newly-created to give experienced NCOs, like Michael, platoon command responsibilities that would, in peace time, normally be the preserve of commissioned officers. Michael took command of three platoons in B Company as the 2nd Battalion received orders to sail for France as part of the 8th Infantry Brigade of General Montgomery's 3rd Division of the British Expeditionary Force (BEF), leaving Gosport on 28 September 1939 and reaching Cherbourg the next day. From there the battalion was taken by train to its designated Gondecourt (59) sector south-west of Lille and close to the Belgian border. In November the battalion moved to Roubaix where, apart from the occasional appearance of an enemy reconnaissance aircraft, the so-called 'Phoney War' gave little cause for concern. A return to Gondecourt saw the battalion digging defence trenches, locating sites for fixed gun positions, carrying out training and keeping fit by a programme of sports activities. Thanks to his French language skills, Michael played a lead role in liaising with the local communities and made several friends among the French, especially with the Pachy family in Gondecourt.

The war's first Christmas and the New Year of 1940 were celebrated in France under this seemingly unreal state of war, but all changed with the German invasion of Holland and Belgium. The latter being only a few kilometres away from where Michael and his unit were based, the battalion quickly moved forward, crossing the Franco-Belgian border and taking up defensive positions in the town of Louvain, the 8th Infantry Brigade having been ordered to stop the German advance. This was now nothing 'phoney' about the conflict. Michael and his men were repeatedly strafed and harassed by enemy aircraft and patrols frequently clashed with German advance units. An attempt by the British infantry to advance on the night of 23 May 1940 was beaten back by superior enemy fire power and the BEF's left flank, to the coast, was then left unguarded when the Belgian forces holding it unconditionally surrendered on 28 May 1940. The battalion had no option but to join the remaining BEF in fighting a rear guard action towards the coast and, hopefully, evacuation to England. Michael and his men therefore fell back, first to Poperinghe and then to Furnes [Veurne] where two platoons took up position around an old farmhouse and engaged in a bitter exchange of fire with German forces in a neighbouring village. Only with difficulty was Michael able to withdraw his men and continue their retreat, rejoining the remainder of B Company on the beach at Dunkirk. It was there that enemy aircraft bombed and machine-gunned the unit and, although he was successfully evacuated, Michael received a head wound, which necessitated a six weeks' stay in hospital back in England.

When recovered, Michael learned that he was to receive a Mention in Despatches for his courage and leadership during the retreat to Dunkirk. He was also recommended for a commission and was therefore posted to Aldershot, to the 170th Officer Cadet Training Unit (170 OCTU) which specialised in training machine gun officers. He passed the two-month course, but as was normal practice for officers newly-commissioned from the ranks, he was not able to rejoin the Middlesex Regiment and was instead posted in January 1941 as a Second Lieutenant, with the service number 167302, to the Manchester Regiment and its machine gun training centre at Ladysmith Barracks in Ashton-under-Lyne, Lancashire.

Trotobas was lucky to escape from the beaches at Dunkirk. Photo: author's coll.

But before Michael could take up duties with his new regiment, he was summoned in mid-March 1941 for a War Office interview, his language skills and knowledge of France having been brought to the attention of SOE. He was security-cleared by MI5 on 2 April 1941 and by 17 April he was a member of Party 27D undergoing preliminary training and assessment at STS 5, Wanborough Manor.

At STS 5 there were contradictory reports on Trotobas. He was judged keen, inventive and quick thinking, but as a result of his previous experience in the army and in action the conclusion of Major Douglas Larder, Wanborough's commandant at the time, included the observation:

'This officer is inclined to be slack, owing to the fact that he knows his subjects'.

The staff also noted an antipathy between Trotobas and another trainee agent in Party 27D, Lieutenant George Langelaan, similarly strong-willed and with previous experience in the British Army. Overall, however, Trotobas was described as good natured and a good mixer in the group and he had no difficulty in being passed at Wanborough in order to continue with the next phase of his training.

Trotobas clashed with another trainee at STS 5, Lieutenant George Langelaan – pictured here after facial alterations to provide a disguise for his clandestine service in France. Photo: author's coll.

His training syllabus continued with a Group A paramilitary training course and for this Trotobas went on with the other successful members of Party 27D to STS 25a, Garramor House, near Arisaig in Inverness-shire. Again, Trotobas received conflicting reports, though this may have been at least partly due to the confusion as to the type of future role he might carry out. Several appreciative comments suggest that he was seen as a potential leader for a *coup de main* party (though his map reading was criticised), but he was found wanting in the clandestine arts of codes, ciphers and propaganda. The summary of Lieutenant-Colonel Munn, officer commanding at STS 25a, read:

> 'Trotobas has guts and determination. Moderate intelligence but extremely keen. Has shown slight tendency to be impulsive and has given the impression of being opinionated......'.

His personal file holds no record of his further training but Trotobas would next have taken his parachute training course at STS 51, RAF Ringway, which he completed successfully. He would then have attended a Group B Finishing School course at Beaulieu in the New Forest, most probably at STS 31, 'The House in the Wood'. With his training completed, he was designated to become a circuit leader and his orders were to go to southern France and recruit and establish a circuit in the unoccupied zone.

He was dropped from a 138 Squadron Whitley, flown by Flight Sergeant Reimer, on 6 September 1941, one of a group of six agents, the others being George Langelaan (UKELELE/

Langdon), Ben Cowburn (BLACKTHORN/*Benoît*), André Bloch (DRAFTSMAN/*Georges 9*) and Comte Jean du Puy (*Camille*), all of French Section, together with Victor Gerson, an agent of SOE's DF Section. The group dropped to a pre-arranged reception committee on the farmland of Auguste Chantraine at Tendu (36) near Châteauroux, and Trotobas then made his way to Marseilles where he met, as instructed, another French Section agent, Captain Gilbert Turck (*Christophe*) at a well-used safe house, the Villa des Bois. Turck was to help Trotobas settle into the area, but after only a month in France, Trotobas was arrested when he returned to Châteauroux to try to make contact with the French Section radio operator, Georges Bégué (BOMBPROOF/*Georges 1*). The 'letter box' for making contact and leaving messages in Châteauroux was at the garage of a man named Fleuret and it was there on 10 October 1941 that Trotobas arranged to meet Bégué's courier, locally-recruited Jean Bougennec (later BUTLER/*Max*). Unbeknown to both, Fleuret had been arrested and the Vichy police were now keeping watch on the garage as a '*souricière*', a 'mouse trap', in order to catch other agents and helpers calling there. Within minutes of each other, Trotobas and Bougennec were captured as the police sprang their trap. There seemed no point in denial, so Trotobas admitted his identity as an agent, was charged with activities contrary to the interests of Vichy France, and sent to the notorious Maison d'Arrêt prison in the place Belleyme in Périgueux, a penal institution for serious offenders. The prison's notoriety came from its conditions: it was filthy; ill-served in respect of sanitation; and prone to infestations of lice. The prisoners were, however, free to mix in the communal areas and Trotobas found himself in the company of a large group of SOE agents and their helpers who had been arrested. In similar fashion to the '*souricière*' operated at the Fleuret garage, the Vichy French police had set up a similar trap at the Villa des Bois supposed safe house in Marseilles and had netted several more French Section agents and supporters in what was a major disaster for SOE.

Trotobas was first imprisoned in the Maison d'Arrêt prison in Périgueux. Photo: author.

Fortunately, the agents' stay at Périgueux was not too long since, in March 1942 and following pressure from the US Consulate, the SOE prisoners were moved *en bloc* to the internment camp at Mauzac, where conditions were markedly better. Red Cross parcels arrived and the SOE group, quickly in league with other influential prisoners who supported the Allied cause, began to plot a mass break-out. In preparation for this, Trotobas led a programme of fitness training, while Georges Bégué, another of those captured, masterminded the break-out plan by establishing contact with London via a clandestine radio that was smuggled into the camp. With the outside help of the wife of one of the prisoners, and the escape line set up by Victor Gerson who had parachuted into France at the same time as Trotobas, all preparations for their evasion were completed and on 15 July 1942, only three months after their arrival at Mauzac, Trotobas and his fellow-conspirators escaped.

The camp at Mauzac. Photo: author's coll.

Gerson's escape organisation hid them until the anticipated police activity abated and while they were issued with new false identity cards. They were then moved on, via Oullins (69), to Lyons. There they were divided into two groups for the remainder of the escape route to Spain. Trotobas was in what was to be the second group to leave Lyons, consisting of himself, Langelaan, three Frenchmen who had worked with SOE - Robert Lyon, Philippe Liewer and Jean Bougennec (arrested with Trotobas at the Fleuret garage) and one of Mauzac's guards, Anton Sevilla, who had been a critical element in aiding the escape and in return had asked to be taken with the escapees to England.

The second group left Lyons on 28 August 1942, making their way by train via Narbonne to Perpignan. There, they took a taxi to a rendez-vous with a Spanish guide who led them through the Pyrenees mountains into the safety of neutral Spain. Once over the border, Langelaan collapsed from the exhaustion of the mountain crossing, which had taken a day and two nights of painful walking in inadequate footwear. The others continued, but were abandoned on the outskirts of Figueras when their guide took their watches, supposedly to sell in return for food, but disappeared. Undeterred, Trotobas and his remaining four

Trotobas, (right) centre with legs apart and (below), eighth from left, pictured among prisoners at Mauzac. Photos: Danièle Lhereux coll. and author's coll.

companions set off to follow the railway line by night to Girona, some 40 kilometres away. They split up on the way, but all subsequently reached Girona and went on to the British Consulate in Barcelona. Lyon and Liewer arrived first, followed a week later by Bougennec and then Trotobas, both of whom had been delayed by stomach problems. Sevilla arrived shortly afterwards and the five then learned that the first group of six evaders had all been arrested by the Spanish police and imprisoned in the internment camp at Miranda del Ebro, also well-known for its harsh conditions and regime. Langelaan, likewise arrested after he had been left behind by the second group, was also sent to Miranda.

From Barcelona, Trotobas was in a first group of three, together with Bougennec and Liewer, driven to Madrid by diplomatic car and then on to Lisbon in Portugal where they were temporarily placed in protective custody while awaiting passage to England. This was to be a priority movement by air and on 16 September 1942 they flew by BOAC Short Empire flying boat to Poole, from where they were taken up to SOE headquarters in London for debriefing.

Trotobas was returned to England in the comparative luxury of a BOAC Short Empire flying boat. Photo: author's coll.

The mistakes that had led to the arrest of so many agents were an embarrassment to SOE and it was clear that those early agents sent had been ill-prepared and trained, especially with regard to the eventuality of being arrested. In his two months back in Britain, Trotobas would therefore undoubtedly have received more instruction or at least a detailed re-briefing. His SOE file holds no details of this, yet it is clear that he quickly agreed to go back to France to again set up a circuit, but in an area with which he was far more familiar and comfortable – Lille, in the north of the country, where he had served in the B.E.F. Equally to his liking was the role designated for the circuit, since preparation for sabotage of the enemy's industrial and transport facilities was to be a priority.

For this second mission, Trotobas was given the code name FARMER, which was therefore to also be the codename of his circuit, the field name *Sylvestre* and the false identity of Joseph Rampal. He was to be sent with a radio operator, Lieutenant Arthur Staggs (BAKER/*Guy*) and both were to be dropped 'blind', i.e. without a reception committee, with Major Gustave Biéler (MUSICIAN/*Guy*) a Canadian agent of French Section also on his way to northern France.

For his second mission, Trotobas was dropped into France with a W/T operator, Lieutenant Arthur Staggs (left) and, heading for a separate mission, Major Guy Biéler. Photos: author's coll and Jacqueline Biéler.

The three men were dropped on the night of 18/19 November 1942 from the Whitley of Flight Lieutenant Prior DFM and his crew of 161 Squadron, from RAF Tempsford. Their DZ was not in northern France, due to the strong German forces, both ground and air, present there, but was instead in the Loiret region near Gondreville (45) some 25 kilometres north-west of Montargis (45). The flight to France was a foretaste of the drama to come. From Tempsford, Prior set his course to make a French landfall at Cabourg, but a change in wind direction took him over the heavily-defended port of Le Havre at an altitude of only 2,400 feet. Enemy flak opened up from all sides, providing what must have been an unsettling experience for the agents inside the Whitley. While the aircraft somehow escaped unscathed, a further concern developed as the aircraft's starboard engine began losing power. Despite hazy visibility, Prior successfully identified the distinctive bend in the Loire river south of Orléans and then picked up a railway line to follow to the drop zone. Trotobas and Staggs landed without incident, but Biéler landed on rocky ground and sustained a severe injury to his back. Despite being in great pain, Biéler managed to keep up with Trotobas and Staggs in a cross-country hike to the train station of Auxy-Juranville from where they caught the early morning train to the capital, 100 kilometres to the north.

In Paris their orders were to first contact Major Francis Suttill (PHYSICIAN/*Prosper*) who was to help Biéler contact the CARTE resistance organisation in the south of France, with the aim of developing a northern branch of CARTE. He was also to help Trotobas and Staggs on their way to Lille, but Biéler's injury was soon confirmed as serious and would necessitate his staying in the capital for treatment and convalescence. It was therefore only Trotobas and Staggs who, having been held for a few days at separate safe houses, then met Suttill at 38 avenue de Suffren, the home of the two Tambour sisters, Germaine and Madeleine, who ran a safe house for the PHYSICIAN

38 avenue de Suffren, home of the Tambour sisters Germaine and Madeleine. Photos: author and Danièle Lhereux coll.

network. It was agreed that Biéler could, at least temporarily, no longer carry out his mission, but that Trotobas should continue on to Lille as ordered. One obstacle to this was that Staggs was as yet unable to get his radio set to work, much to the annoyance and frustration of Trotobas and adding to the tense relationship that had already developed between the two men. Trotobas had to rely on Suttill's W/T operator, Gilbert Norman (BUTCHER/*Archambaud*) to send his messages to London and he left Staggs behind when he went on to Lille. There, he was fortunate to quickly make the acquaintance of a local man, Victor Emmanuel 'Manu' Lemercier, who agreed not only to help him, but also to give him lodgings and to find accommodation for Staggs when the latter came to Lille.

Once settled in Lille, Trotobas began to develop membership of his circuit, accepting several relatives and friends of Lemercier and making contact with local French people who he had met while with the BEF in France in 1940 and whom he judged still likely to be sympathetic to the Allied cause. The FARMER circuit grew rapidly and efficiently, recruiting helpers in identified key areas of the community, transportation, local industry and the authorities. It also grew geographically beyond Lille, around Valenciennes and, to the west, to St. Omer, Abbeville and as far as Dunkirk on the coast. FARMER cells were even created in Belgium, including a group of customs officers on the border.

Major Francis Suttill (left) and his W/T operator Major Gilbert Norman supported Trotobas on his arrival in Paris. Photos: author's coll.

To equip all his circuit members with the arms and sabotage material that they needed, Trotobas required reliable communication with London, in order to arrange air drops of supplies. But though Staggs had joined him, his radio set was still not functioning and he could not raise London. This did little to improve the antipathy between Staggs and Trotobas, nor did it impress FARMER's new recruits. To get around the problem, it was necessary to use Suttill's W/T operators in Paris, but this required visits by Trotobas or the tiresome use of couriers to and from the capital. This situation was then exacerbated by bad weather over the winter of 1942/43, which made air operations problematic and it was not until April 1943 that Trotobas received his first drop of weapons and explosives. This event, and the other drops that were to follow, were long overdue in that, since November 1942 when the Germans had taken over the previously unoccupied zone, SOE had issued fresh instructions that sabotage could go ahead, rather than wait for the invasion. This was exactly the type of order for which Trotobas had been eagerly waiting. His enthusiasm was not dented by the decision of Staggs, still at odds with him and still unable to operate his W/T set, to leave the circuit at the end of March 1943 and to go to live with a boyhood friend in Roubaix. The departure of Staggs was more than compensated for by the arrival of Pierre Séailles, recently released from Mauzac prison where he had met and befriended Trotobas in the spring of 1942. But this important addition to the circuit created a new tension, for Trotobas chose to make Séailles his second-in-command, displacing Lemercier who had effectively carried out that role since FARMER was established. Trotobas had become godfather to the Lemerciers' newly-born son and Lemercier was deeply hurt by what he deemed to be Trotobas' lack of confidence in him. To make matters worse, Séailles did not take to Lemercier and, over time, began to suspect that the latter was giving information to the enemy (a fear that was never proven against Lemercier) and selling and mis-using false identity cards produced for the circuit.

Pierre Séailles (left) eventually replaced Manu Lemercier as the deputy to Trotobas. Lemercier is pictured with his wife and son, Michel, godson of, and named after, Trotobas. Photos: Brigitte Seailles coll. and Danièle Lhereux coll.

As the arms drops continued, a steady flow of intelligence on potential targets came in to FARMER, including details of enemy airfields, U-boat bases, supply movements, factories and power supplies. Using this information, sabotage operations began from May 1943, initiated by railway workers in Lille and Valenciennes who blew up petrol trains and loco-motives and started misdirecting trains carrying enemy vehicles, aircraft and equipment. It was then the following month that Trotobas and the FARMER circuit achieved their most spectacular sabotage act, following a specific request from SOE headquarters. The target was the extensive locomotive construction and repair facility of SNCF, the French national rail company. Located in the Fives district of Lille, close to the city centre, it had already been the subject of four bombing raids by the RAF – all to no avail and resulting in many civilian casualties and a great deal of destruction to domestic property. To prevent further such impact on the local population, SOE asked if the works might be put out of use by sabotage and Trotobas willingly agreed to an attempt, carrying out a personal reconnaissance of the works in the company of one of his volunteers who worked there. The attack was set for 26 June 1943 and Trotobas assembled a group of both real and false police, with the ingenious plan of bluffing his way into the works on the pretext that the police had been alerted to a report of saboteurs targeting the plant. At a late stage in planning, he was joined by Lieutenant François Reeve (CARDINAL/*Olivier*) who had been dropped into the Touraine region on 13 June 1943 with orders to make his way north to Lille and join Trotobas as a sabotage instructor. His arrival was not greeted with good grace by Trotobas as the latter was still in need of a reliable W/T set and operator and felt himself adequately served by his own sabotage skills and those of several of his helpers whom he had trained. Nevertheless, Reeve's specialised training was not to be ignored and he therefore took part in the action on the night of 26 June. Accompanied by a German-speaking helper dressed in enemy uniform as a Colonel, the group had no difficulty in hoodwinking the factory's security personnel and were gone in little more than 30 minutes. As they made good their escape they were rewarded with the sound of the explosives detonating, creating damage that reportedly kept the works out of commission for two months.

Lieutenant François Reeve, a sabotage specialist, joined Trotobas in June 1943. Photo: TNA.

The success at Fives heralded a series of sabotage operations over the coming months, but it also made the Germans determined to catch a man they knew by the same name as that used by the French *Résistance* – '*Capitaine Michel*'. A number of arrests led to information being revealed by prisoners under duress and as a precaution, Trotobas and a woman helper who had become his girlfriend, Denise Gilman, changed their appearance and moved to new lodgings in Lille. They were given the first floor of the house, 74 rue Caumartin, of Madame Chardin, recently-widowed and a trustworthy helper of FARMER. They moved there on 18 August 1943 and as a further safeguard a helper of Trotobas, who was a local police commander, arranged for him to receive the false identity and uniform of an Inspector in the *Groupes Mobiles de Réserve*, the Vichy French reserve police force, the GMR. With this additional layer of protection, Trotobas felt able to pick up his own activity again, knowing it was important to be seen to be leading from the front. On 2 October 1943 he mounted a lone foray against the Fives works, destroying one of two cranes that he had made his target. His extended FARMER network carried on with a continuous programme of sabotage, chiefly against railway targets such turntables, signal boxes and cranes such as the ones that Trotobas had attacked at Fives.

Denise Gilman became the close companion of Trotobas. Photo: Danièle Lhereux coll.

Trotobas frequently changed identity, and his looks, to keep the Germans off his trail. Photos: Danièle Lhereux coll.

The leadership tensions in the circuit had been temporarily resolved by the transfer of Lemercier to the Pas de Calais area, on the promise of being got out to England, thereby allowing Séailles to continue as lieutenant to Trotobas in and around Lille. Another command problem had arisen in that recently-arrived Reeve, like Staggs, did not hit it off with Trotobas and frequently challenged his authority to the extent that the two men eventually came to blows. Trotobas, the former army boxing champion, easily re-asserted his leadership. None of this, however, endeared Reeve to the chief local French helpers of

FARMER, they considered Reeve to be a braggart, unpredictable and lacking in security awareness. Trotobas partly solved this by sending Reeve to be based in Arras to take charge of a branch of FARMER that was active there, but according to local French sources, this semi-independence only increased Reeve's own opinion of himself.

Matters came to a head when Lemercier, concerned that he had been side-lined and his departure to England had not been arranged, returned on a visit to Lille in mid-October. Looking up those local Frenchmen who had risen in the circuit while he had been sidelined, he complained bitterly that if he were not taken out to England he might soon be arrested (the Germans had his name and description) and could then reveal their identities and whereabouts. The French, shocked and dismayed, recommended to Trotobas that Lemercier was now too much of a liability and a danger and that he should be executed. But Trotobas, godfather to Lemercier's son, felt a duty to the man who had helped him so much in the early days of the FARMER circuit. He instead assured his senior lieutenants that Lemercier had only been sounding off through frustration and that a quiet word from Trotobas would put him straight. Lemercier returned to Bruay in the Pas de Calais and stayed there until, at the end of October, Trotobas collected him, brought him to Lille and then had him escorted to Arras in preparation for his despatch, via an escape line, to Spain and then on to England. But while Lemercier waited in Arras, a series of arrests broke up the escape line and on 3 November 1943 matters took a dramatic turn.

According to local French sources Reeve, still in charge in Arras, was furious that the arrests were due to a man (Woussen) whom he had wanted executed, but had subsequently been captured while attempting to reach Spain. He saw his own opinion, rather than that of Trotobas and his other lieutenants, vindicated and he now resolved that the other danger, Lemercier, should be removed. Calling for Lemercier to be taken to an isolated house, Reeve followed and according to the Frenchmen present, entered the property and, as Lemercier's back was turned, shot him the back of the neck, killing him instantly. Two local helpers helped Reeve dispose of the body by throwing it into a disused well.

In Reeve's later report, however, he claimed that Trotobas decided upon and carried out the shooting, and that Reeve was only involved by way of removing papers from the body and arranging for its disappearance down the well. Given Reeve's subsequent actions and behaviour, the balance of probability seems heavily weighted in favour of the account of local French members of FARMER.

Irrespective of the Lemercier affair, sabotage operations continued apace, still largely against railway targets. The Germans went to the extent of publicising, in local French newspapers, these acts which they termed 'terrorism' and stepped up their efforts to locate and capture 'Capitaine Michel'. Their breakthrough came from the capture of the circuit member, Woussens, whom Reeve had wanted to execute. In a domino effect of denouncements and arrests, the trail led back to Arras where, on the night of 26 November, Reeve and a helper were arrested in a raid by the German secret military police – the Geheime Feldpolizei, led by Inspektor Lynen who was in charge of finding Trotobas and destroying the FARMER circuit.

Accounts vary as to the chain of events that followed, but Reeve survived the war to report and admit that he did provide the Germans with the address of Trotobas at

20 boulevard de Belfort to where he had moved from the rue Caumartin. In doing so, however, he claimed that Trotobas had told him a few days earlier that he was moving his lodgings again, so Reeve did not expect him to still be there when the Germans hurried from Arras to Lille, with Reeve present in one of their vehicles. In the boulevard de Belfort the landlady, Madame Mahieu, had already left the house to go to work on the morning of 27 November 1943. Trotobas had dressed in his GMR uniform and with his girlfriend Denise Gilman, was in a first floor bedroom. But as the Germans quietly threw up a cordon around the area at 6.45 a.m. a German soldier emerged from his billet only a few doors away around the corner in the rue Kellerman, carrying his rifle. Mistaken for Trotobas or one of his men by a member of Lynen's squad, he was immediately shot and killed by his fellow Germans. Realising the element of surprise was lost, Lynen ordered his men to break into the flat. Charging up the stairs, they kicked open the door to Trotobas' lodgings, but found their man, in the 'Die hard' tradition of his former unit, the Middlesex Regiment, facing them and armed. Trotobas fired first, killed the German NCO who led the break-in, and seriously wounding another. But the remaining enemy soldiers returned fire with a hail of sub-machine gun bullets, killing Trotobas instantly and mortally wounding Denise Gillman who died some 30 minutes later from an agonising stomach wound. Ironically, Lynen was at first not convinced that he had his man. Trotobas had changed his appearance since that last known to the Germans, he was wearing the uniform of an Inspector in the Vichy police reserve and had yet another new identity, of Robert Lesage. Lynen therefore had Reeve brought to the house where it was confirmed that the dead man was indeed '*Capitaine Michel*'. Trotobas had indeed 'died hard'.

Trotobas was shot and killed at 20 boulevard de Belfort on the morning of 27 November 1943. A plaque commemorates Trotobas and Denise Gilman who died with him. Photos: author.

To make doubly sure, Lynen nevertheless had Trotobas' body first taken to Calmette Hospital where it was cleaned up before several other captured members of the FARMER circuit were brought, one by one over the next few days, to confirm the dead man's identity. Eventually satisfied that it was indeed Trotobas who had been killed, Lynen released the body to the civil authorities with the strict order that a burial was to be arranged in secrecy, in an unmarked grave. The job was passed to the central police station in Lille where FARMER had several officers committed to the cause. As a result, a strong police escort, composed entirely of men loyal to Trotobas, accompanied the coffin for burial in the Lille-Sud cemetery.

Trotobas was buried in Lille-Sud cemetery. Photos: author.

One of the great ironies of the wartime service of Michael Trotobas is that, despite being recommended by SOE for a posthumous Victoria Cross (VC), Britain's highest decoration for valour in combat, he received no recognition at all. The VC application was turned down as not meeting the criterion of having been witnessed by a senior officer and in the administrative turmoil of SOE being wound down at the end of the war, a re-application for a lesser award was overlooked. Despite the high esteem in which he had been held in France (his grave was the scene an annual Anglo-French commemoration event for many years) he similarly received no award from the French government. His courage and achievements live on, however, in the naming of roads in northern France (in Lille, Loos, Wasquehal, Mons-en-Baroeul and Mouvaux) honouring *'Capitaine Michel'*.

Three of the roads named after Trotobas/*Capitaine Michel*. Photos: author.

Sources and acknowledgements: the SOE personal file of Michael Trotobas is (TNA) HS9/1487/1. The French historian Danièle Lheureux, wrote of Trotobas and his circuit in *La Résistance "Action-Buckmaster" SYLVESTRE-FARMER avec le capitaine "Michel"*, published in 2001 (ISBN 2-914670-01-X). The comprehensive and recommended biography of Trotobas, '*Agent Michael Trotobas and SOE in Northern France*', Pen and Sword, 2015 ISBN 978-1-47385—163-4) provided much detail in the above account, with the generous co-operation of the authors Stewart Kent and Nick Nicholas.

CHAPTER 7

CAPTAIN EDWARD ZEFF
MBE CROIX DE GUERRE
FRENCH SECTION

Photo: TNA

EDWARD ZEFF WAS BORN INTO A BRITISH JEWISH FAMILY AT 22 HANOVER

Crescent, Brighton on 22 April 1904. Also known as Ted or Eddie, he was the youngest of the three children of Simon and Hannah Zeff. His sister was also called Hannah, though known as "Queenie", and his brother was Abraham, "Braham", also known as "Bray". The Zeff family had first come to England with the arrival of Edward's grandfather, Abraham Hersz Zaif in the 1870s, fleeing persecution in Kalisz, in a Russian-annexed area of Poland. A tailor by trade, Abraham Zaif settled in the then predominantly-Jewish area of Whitechapel in east London, making waterproof clothing. In 1886 the family became naturalised British under the name of Zeff and Abraham's three sons, Harris, Simon (Edward's father) and Wolfe, followed the family career path and became tailors. The family business prospered and moved from Whitechapel to Croydon in Surrey and then, by 1900, to Brighton in Sussex. Simon, a Master Tailor, married a Brighton girl, Hannah ("Annie") Hyams, and continued to work in the family business of A. Zeff, firstly at 159 North Street while the family lived at Hanover Crescent and then at 40 North Street, Brighton. Brighton at that time had the fifth largest Jewish population in Britain and was especially popular for holidays among London's Jewish community. The Zeff family soon established itself in Brighton and Simon Zeff became the Chairman of the Brighton and Hove Jewish Board of Guardians.

Zeff was born at 22 Hanover Crescent, Brighton. Photo: Malcolm, Conor and Lucas Hatch.

The Zeff family's commercial premises included, above left, 159 North Street (Hair Mechanics) and, right, 40 North Street. Photos: Simon Carey.

Edward attended the former York Place Elementary Schools in York Place/Pelham Street, Brighton, but when the school buildings were used as an Indian military hospital during the First World War (while Edward was a pupil) the children were temporarily relocated and taught at the Technical College in Richmond Terrace. After Edward had completed his schooling, the York Place buildings were later taken over by the Technical College, subsequently Brighton College of Technology and now City College, Brighton & Hove.

The former York Place Elementary Schools in Brighton. Photo: author's collection.

Edward's brother, Braham, started his own tailoring business in Paris from around 1922 and Edward subsequently joined him. In 1928 Edward opened up a branch of the business at 24 rue de la Pépinière in the 8e *arrondissement* of the city. The shop was on the ground floor of new premises built only the year before on the site of a former military barracks, the Caserne de la Pépinière. With its main facade on the place Saint-Augustin, the building was a landmark development in the neo-classical style, creating on the ground floor at 8 place Saint-Augustin and on the first floor throughout, the *Cercle National des Armées de Terre, de Mer et de l'Air*, a club, restaurant and hotel for officers of the French armed forces. The Zeffs' establishments became known for specialising in fashionable menswear, including silk shirts, dressing gowns, gentlemen's hosiery and haberdashery. Braham had married in 1927 and Edward followed suit in 1930 when he married Reine Sevilla, a Frenchwoman born into the Parisian Jewish community.

After the fall of France, Edward elected to come to England with his wife, while Braham decided to remain in France with his wife and his son, Daniel, despite the inevitability of internment as a foreign alien, or worse, given that they were Jewish. Appreciating that he had detailed knowledge of France and the language, Edward offered himself for special duties, via a Colonel Jeffes, in February 1941, but in the meantime had enlisted in the Royal Corps of Signals on 6 March 1941 as a Signalman, with the service number 2366392. He joined the 1st Operators Training Battalion (OTB) at Catterick Camp in Yorkshire, being described, somewhat unflatteringly, as a short, stocky man with fair balding hair. He was then interviewed by French Section of SOE and security-cleared by MI5 on 15 September 1941.

Above - The *Cercle National des Armées de Terre, de Mer et de l'Air* in Paris. Zeff's shop in the rue de la Pépinière was on the right-hand frontage of the building. Photo: author's collection. Today, (right) it is a women's clothing shop, *Sienne*. Photo: Dr Chris Warne.

As a precautionary measure to protect the Zeff family members still in France, Edward was given a false name with the same initials, Eugène Zoltan, before undertaking his training. A member of Party 27J, he first went to the Preliminary School at STS 5, Wanborough Manor, on 3 October 1941 and performing well despite initially displaying a lack of self-confidence. He was judged strong, agile and athletic and worked well at the courses, leading Major Roger de Wesselow, STS 5's commandant, to report:

> 'A cheerful sort of person with a strong sense of humour and extensive knowledge of the world. Popular. Has his ups and downs. Cute, courageous and reliable. A really good type of *commerçant*'.

Though his SOE personal file contains no details, he would have continued with Party 27J for paramilitary training in Scotland, at one of the Group A schools near Arisaig in Inverness-shire, almost certainly STS 25 at Garramor House, Morar. By his successful completion of the course there, it was confirmed that Zeff was best suited to becoming a W/T operator and he was commissioned in the General List on 30 November 1941 as a Second Lieutenant with the new service number 221219. He would therefore have next attended STS 52 at Thame Park, Oxfordshire for his radio work training, his file containing a note that his 'scheme' took place in February 1942. For this exercise he went to, and transmitted from, Swansea where he lodged with a Mrs Halliday who took him to be French. It is unclear as to whether Zeff was parachute-trained, nor is there any record of attendance at a Group B Finishing School at Beaulieu in the New Forest, though other members of Party 27J graduated from STS 31, The Rings.

During his training, Zeff had come to know another young British Jewish W/T operator of French Section, Isidore Newman. They were paired to both be inserted by sea into unoccupied Vichy France and in preparation for that they first travelled together by train to the airfield at Whitchurch near Bristol, from where they were flown to Gibraltar on 2 March 1942. At this relatively early stage of SOE's operations, French Section normally used the names of trees for code names and a numbered variant of *Georges* as the field name for radio operators. For his mission, Zeff was therefore given the code name EBONY and the field name *Georges 53,* with a false identity as Etienne Pierre Pascal.

Zeff, visually transformed to support his false French identity of Etienne Pascal. Photo: Zeff collection.

Landings on the southern coast of France were undertaken by either fishing boat or submarine, both types being based at Gibraltar and Zeff and Newman were to constitute half of a group of four agents to be landed in two separate locations by submarine. They left Gibraltar in HM Submarine *Unbroken* – P42, commanded by Lieutenant Alastair Mars, in early April. Space on the submarine was already at a premium, so the addition of four agents and a Conducting Officer, Captain Peter Churchill, made for extremely cramped conditions on the voyage. The landing was to be undertaken from two collapsible canoes, 'folboats', that the submarine carried, and when the designated spot was reached off the French coast near Antibes on the night of 19/20 April, Churchill paddled one, and Zeff and Newman the other, to the beach. While the two agents waited, Churchill located the safe house in Antibes that the agents were to go to, the Villa des Bois of Dr. Louis Lévy. As Churchill then returned to the beach to ensure that the W/T sets and suitcases of Zeff and Newman were safely ashore, Lévy and a small group of helpers arrived at the landing spot to assist. Bidding them all farewell, Churchill paddled back to the submarine while Zeff and Newman were taken up to the villa.

HM Submarine *Unbroken* and above, its captain, Lieutenant Alastair Mars. Photos: author's collection.

Zeff's orders required him to take the train from Antibes, carrying his W/T set with him in a suitcase, and to go to Lyons where he was to report to one of French Section's most successful agents, Virginia Hall. An American journalist based in Lyons, Hall made good use of her professional cover and her status as a 'neutral' (the USA still maintained diplomatic relations with Vichy France) to work for the British and SOE and from the earliest days of French Section's clandestine activity, she acted as a central point through which many agents passed, made contact or sought help.

After his arrival in Lyons, Zeff was to work with French Section's Lieutenant Georges Duboudin (SPRUCE, later PLAYWRIGHT/*Alain*), but his first contact failed and it was only after a delay of a few days that he managed to get in touch directly with Virginia Hall. He arranged his own lodgings in the rue Camille in the suburb of Montchat, some seven kilometres from the city centre and, thanks to being provided with a good protection team, felt confident enough to always transmit from the same house – though this was contrary to SOE's standing instruction for W/T operators to vary their location for transmissions. The risk taken was exacerbated by the fact that Zeff, once he had settled into his role, was required to handle so much radio traffic, he transmitted at least three times a week, sometimes for up to six hours a day. He was praised for his radio work by Duboudin, doubtless grateful that Zeff carried out all coding and decoding himself and, as time allowed, assisted with the other activities of the SPRUCE circuit, such as helping evaders and escapees and arranging receptions for agent/arms drops. At the beginning of May, Zeff also helped his circuit leader to hide and to then again take up the reins of SPRUCE after Duboudin had been arrested, but later released, by a sympathetic French police officer.

In August Zeff was visited by Nicholas Bodington, second-in-command of French Section, who had come to Lyons to investigate and try to resolve a number of tensions that had developed among French Section's personnel in the city. These tensions included a negative report by Zeff on Duboudin and his complaint about Virginia Hall's authoritative ways. As a result of the meeting, Zeff was judged in need of a break and therefore went to Toulouse and Avignon, in theory to operate for another circuit organiser, but in reality for respite from the tensions of his work. When he returned to Lyons later in the year, he was supposed to again link up with Virginia Hall, but the latter had had to rapidly leave Lyons as a result of the German take-over of the *Zone Libre* in November 1942. Instead, Zeff met again with another of French Section's agents, Robert Boiteux (GARDENER/*Nicolas*), who had taken over much of Duboudin's work when the latter had been recalled to England in October 1942. Boiteux's own W/T operator, Pierre Le Chêne (ASPEN/*Grégoire*) was arrested in November and Boiteux therefore welcomed the chance to maintain radio contact with England via Zeff. In contrast to the earlier antipathies among the Lyons-based F Section agents, Zeff and Boiteux hit it off immediately, Boiteux subsequently recalling:

> 'I liked Zeff. He was frank and accepted without any qualms the double risk he ran of being a British agent "pianist" [W/T operator] and a Jew. As he said: "They can only kill me for one or the other!"'.

Above: (left to right) F Section agents Isidore Newman, Virginia Hall, Georges Duboudin and Robert Boiteux. Photos: TNA; author's coll; Tony Duboudin and Evelyn Le Chêne coll.

For the next few months Zeff supported Boiteux and his GARDENER circuit. He lived outside the city, but transmitted from a house in the centre where he was protected by a team of helpers and was visited each day by Boiteux. He helped in the escape of Bob Sheppard (PALM/*Patrice*) a French Section agent who had been captured immediately after landing by the Vichy police. Sheppard had managed to escape from hospital, but being well-known to the enemy authorities, had to be got out of France. When Zeff sent the messages to make the necessary arrangements, he asked London if he, too, could come out of the field, feeling that he had served long enough and that he was a known and wanted man, whose luck would soon be bound to run out. The enemy's direction-finding activities in Lyons were now extensive and as was recounted by Boiteux in Evelyn Le Chêne's book, *'Watch For Me By Moonlight'* Zeff had already experienced an extremely-narrow escape when, after one transmitting session he:

'was roused by banging at the door and shouts of "Police, open up". He ran down from his flat so that he would be the person to open the door. They were two policemen outside with a very conspicuous Gestapo 'observer', and another policeman in a car with the motor ticking over. "On which floor is the Englishman?" asked one of them, elbowing his way into the doorway. "On the second floor", Zeff replied "but I saw him go out, not ten minutes ago – that way". The police made a quick turn about and went roaring off in the direction indicated. Zeff had just enough time to collect his set and make his getaway before, like maddened bulls, they were back for him'.

Zeff had already changed his false identity in France on at least two occasions, to Edouard Zube and Eugène Morin, but SOE headquarters agreed that he should now be considered '*brûlé*' [literally – 'burnt', compromised] and though Zeff was confident of making his own arrangements to join an escape route to Spain, London insisted that he should accompany Sheppard and accept arrangements made separately by headquarters. Zeff therefore made his way to Perpignan where he made pre-arranged contact with a guide and went by bus with him to Amélie-les-Bains (66) where one night was spent in a hotel. Zeff then found himself in a party of four to be led by the guide across the Pyrenees into Spain. Sheppard was the only other SOE agent in the party, the two others being unknown. But only a few minutes after they set out the next day, they were confronted by two German frontier guards. The group tried to make a run for it, but the enemy opened fire and capture was inevitable. The Germans escorted the four evaders and their guide to Arles-sur-Tech and then back to Amélie-les-Bains, Zeff noticing on the way that the guide seemed over-friendly with their captors and that he disappeared when they reached Amélie. Convinced that the guide had betrayed them, Zeff bitterly regretted having followed London's instructions, rather than making his own arrangements for the border crossing.

The group was held for only a few hours at Amélie and after a brief initial interrogation there, during which Zeff offered a cover story of being a shot-down RAF flyer, the arrested men were taken to the *Citadelle* in Perpignan. Zeff shared a cell there with some ten inmates, including Sheppard, and although he was then interrogated at greater length, he successfully maintained his RAF story and was only asked straightforward questions about his past. On or about 1 March 1943 he was taken from Perpignan by train to Paris and imprisoned in the huge prison at Fresnes, just outside the capital. Sheppard travelled on the same train, but in a separate carriage and the two agents remained optimistic that their true identities would remain unknown to the enemy. No questioning at all took place at Fresnes, but one morning around 1 May 1943 Zeff was suddenly called out and taken to the headquarters of the *Sicherheitsdient* (SD) at 84 avenue Foch in Paris. He was taken before a German in civilian clothing and a French *Commissaire* of police, the former addressing Zeff in American-accented English and suggesting it was known that Zeff was a British agent. He was then taken, wearing dark glasses so he could not see the route, by car to "somewhere more comfortable" which proved to be a large house just off the city's boulevard Suchet. Accompanying the German and the French *Commissaire* was another French policeman, then of the *Brigade Spéciale de Paris,* but formerly of the pre-war Vice Squad in the capital and who had known Zeff and had presumably confirmed his British nationality and real name. In the secluded villa Zeff was then subjected to three days of intensive torture, leading French Section's Intelligence Officer, Vera Atkins, to write in 1946 'He suffered more ill-treatment than any other of our agents'. This treatment included the infamous *'baignade'* treatment of near-drowning in a bath, being hung from the ceiling and beaten, and being stripped of his clothes and kept in a cellar with regular beatings and dousings with cold water. On the third day his interrogators produced a photograph of him with details on the reverse, including the name Zeff and mention of Lyons and Toulouse. Told that the game was up, he was advised to give his true story, but Zeff prevaricated for another two days with a new, but still untrue, tale. As a result, he was taken to another villa in the Bois de Boulogne area of the city where he was subjected to sleep deprivation and what Zeff believed to be the lacing of his food and cigarettes with some sort of drug. This induced a semi-hypnotised state for about two to three hours on each occasion, during which he was subjected to several further sessions of unsuccessful interrogation during which the Germans learned no more.

After about a week Zeff was taken back to Fresnes and after a further week's relative respite there, he was taken daily, for three weeks throughout May 1943, to the avenue Foch for more questioning. This time his inquisitors were both German, including the head of the Paris SD, *SS-Standartenführer* Helmut Knochen. Instead of continuing with torture, the enemy now seemed keen only for Zeff to confirm what they already knew. This included them showing Zeff the Germans' messages between Paris, Lyons and Toulouse concerning his whereabouts and movements, intercepts of his radio traffic, considerable detail of SOE's training schools, and evidence that they knew much about the activities of both Virginia Hall and Robert Boiteux in Lyons. Following these sessions, Zeff was returned to imprisonment in Fresnes, but was taken back to the avenue Foch on one occasion to be confronted with three women and asked to confirm that he had worked with him. All three were indeed known to Zeff and though he initially denied recognising them, the Germans produced damning evidence of their involvement, to the extent that Zeff admitted their support. He also spotted Peter Churchill and Georges Duboudin of French Section in Fresnes or at the avenue Foch, both having been captured on later missions to those that had involved Zeff.

SS Standartenfuhrer Helmut Knochen. Photo: Bundesarchiv. 096-10. Right - SD headquarters in Paris at 84 avenue Foch. Photo: Simon Cooper-Grundy.

On another occasion, Zeff was visited at Fresnes by one of his German interrogators from the avenue Foch. He was told that other arrested agents had agreed to reveal the location of arms dumps in return for treating the relevant captured agents, and their French helpers, as prisoners of war and therefore not liable to execution. Zeff replied that he had not known the locations of arms dumps since, as a W/T operator, this was not something in which he had been involved. The background to this claim by the German was true. It is believed that Major Gilbert Norman (BUTCHER/*Archambaud*) of French Section's PROPSPER circuit, made such a deal with the enemy after he had been captured. This lead to the arrest of many French helpers and the seizure of tons of arms of the PROSPER circuit in and around Paris. The Germans did not keep to their side of the supposed bargain and the majority of those captured were deported to concentration camps in Germany and/or executed.

Zeff was then left alone in Fresnes, fully expecting the order for his execution to arrive at any time until, in November 1943, he was in a party of prisoners, the others being unknown to him, deported by train to Germany and Austria. First stop was the transit and punishment camp at Neue Bremm in Saarbrücken where Zeff was held for 15 days in harsh conditions. He was then sent on to Mauthausen in Austria, some 20 kilometres east of Linz. The route taken was a tortuous one, lasting about a week in total and involving one or two-day stops in prisons en route, at Weimar, Hof, Prague and Linz. Mauthausen was a hill-top concentration camp overlooking the Danube river on one side and with a view of snow-capped mountains on the other. Its main headquarters buildings had been constructed in stone and since it opened in 1938, the camp had gained a dreaded reputation as a result of its regime of brutal forced labour in the adjoining granite quarry.

A number of other SOE agents were sent to Mauthausen and some of those few who survived made detailed reports of the harsh regime there and the fact that Zeff, known to be a Jew as well as a British agent, was singled out for especially harsh treatment. He arrived there on 8 December 1943 and soon found that every sort of racket was practised in the camp, along the lines of criminal gang activity. He later complained that a number of Czech and Polish prisoners ingratiated themselves with their captors and received good jobs as secretaries, administrators and assistants to block chiefs. This meant they had good beds, decent food and the pick of civilian clothing taken from new prisoner arrivals. Some even had batmen to wait on them, and, encouraged by the Germans, participated in the brutal treatment and torture of prisoners. Almost anything could be got by bribery, using money, food or cigarettes as currency. Zeff avoided the attentions of the Czech and Polish collaborators because, he believed, he was known to be a British officer. In the published recollections *('Mauthausen: The History Of A Death Camp')* of another French Section agent imprisoned at Mauthausen, Pierre Le Chêne, there is a description of how one German *kapo* (a trustee inmate, collaborating with the enemy, often by carrying out supervisory or administrative duties) regularly picked on Zeff as both British and a Jew, giving him the unenviable job of being the rear partner in the two-man team that carried latrine buckets, on a pole, up the steep steps out of the quarry. Frequent stumbles on the ascent ensured that Zeff received the spillage from the buckets.

Wartime photograph of prisoners on the steps leading to the granite quarry at Mauthausen – up which Zeff had to carry latrine buckets. Photo: Bundesarchiv 192-269.

The former concentration camp at Mauthausen is well-preserved and open to the public as a memorial site. Photos: author.

On the plus side, Zeff was occasionally able to speak with other SOE agents in the camp, including Bob Sheppard, Albert Guérisse (then under the assumed identity of Pat O'Leary), Brian Stonehouse and Pierre Le Chêne. He also benefitted from sympathetic treatment by a fellow prisoner whom Zeff described as 'the only German who ever helped me during my detention'. This was a political prisoner named Hermann who served as the *Lagerschreiber*, the camp secretary, at Melk, a work camp where Zeff was sent from September 1944 to April 1945. Melk, some 80 kilometres east of Mauthausen, was another concentration camp where hard labour was the daily routine – in this case tunnelling into the local mountains to house

The *Appellplatz* at the Melk sub-camp. Today the site is still used today as a barracks by the Austrian Army. Photo: USHHM.

factories making parts for V2 rockets. Hermann twice engineered Zeff avoiding execution while at Melk, including on one occasion when Zeff received 50 lashes and was taken into the camp's hospital prior to being hanged. The transfer to Melk also meant that Zeff was not added to a group of 47 Allied captured agents who arrived at Mauthausen on or around 1 September and were killed just a few days later. Among the six French Section agents in this group was Isidore Newman, who had landed on the south coast of France with Zeff in April 1942, but had been caught during a second mission in France in March 1944.

Having managed to avoid execution while at Melk, Zeff was among the prisoners transferred back to Mauthausen as Allied forces closed in on the area in early May 1945. On the 5th, units of the US Army liberated the camp, but due to a bureaucratic mix-up, it was not until 11 June 1945 that Zeff was flown back to Britain by the USAAF, followed by apologies from Supreme Headquarters Allied Expeditionary Force (SHAEF) for the delay. He received an initial debriefing two days later, followed by a detailed interview on 18 June 1945 and medical clearance in September. Though signed off from SOE the next month, he initially considered further service by deferring his demobilisation from the British Army. In September 1945 he was interviewed for a position in the Control Commission, the body supporting the military authorities in Germany, and undertook an Army Broadcasting Course in December 1945. The same month, however, Zeff was released from London District of the Army, having been recognised by the British with the award of an MBE (Military), the citation for which concluded:

'This officer's loyalty, steadfastness and devotion to duty are worthy of high praise.

He was later decorated by the French with the *Croix de Guerre avec étoile d'argent* [with silver star] and also received, even after his departure from the British Army, a promotion to Captain, back-dated to April 1942. Though he did not contribute to the proceedings, Zeff followed the trial of former camp officials at Mauthausen, and their subsequent fate, detailed in the chapter on Lieutenant Marcus Bloom. Among the accused was *Obersturmbannführer* Julius Ludorf, commandant at Melk when Zeff was a prisoner there. Ludorf was found guilty and hanged in May 1947.

After leaving the Army, Zeff initially returned to the Brighton and Hove area, the address of he and his wife being shown on his file as 94 Embassy Court, Brighton, in correspondence dated 1943 and 1945. Other addresses for him in the area, connected with his family, included 80 New Church Road, Hove, the home of his parents (Zeff's mother had died in 1940 and his father remarried in 1943), and also later in nearby Carlisle Road, Hove. Subsequently, he returned to Paris, living at 23 rue du Laos in the 15e *arrondissement*, while he continued his business in the same premises at 24 rue de la Pépinière, the shop having been looked after by a manageress in Zeff's absence. He spoke little of his wartime experiences, but to his family members his physical and mental health had been damaged, especially by his interrogations and by his time in concentration camps. He suffered from depression and when in very low moods would occasionally talk about Melk and Mauthausen, recalling that when US troops arrived to liberate the camp, they gave out chocolate to some of the former prisoners, but their bodies were unable to cope with the sudden high sugar content of the chocolate and some survivors fell very ill or even died. His marriage to Reine foundered and she departed for a new life in the United States.

Embassy Court, to where Zeff returned after his release from Mauthausen concentration camp. Photo: author's collection.

Despite his return to France, Zeff was an early member of the Special Forces Club in London, maintaining his membership from Paris. He also kept in contact with a number of those with whom he had served in France, including Robert Boiteux (who emigrated to Australia and changed his name to Robert Burdett) and Pierre Le Chêne. The latter's wife, Evelyn, wrote the story of Boiteux's wartime exploits in her book 'Watch For Me By Moonlight' published in 1973. In it, Boiteux was quoted as saying that, after a two-year battle, Zeff seemed to have beaten throat cancer, but only shortly afterwards, stricken by the disease that had undoubtedly been brought about by his heavy chain-smoking, Zeff died in Paris on 8 June 1973, aged 69, at the Hôpital Curie. As he still held British nationality, his death was notified to the British Consulate in Paris, his occupation being described as hosier on his death certificate.

Sources and acknowledgements: David Armstrong; Martyn Cox; Louisa Russell; Steven Kippax; Christine Miller; Daniel Zeff; Dr Chris Warne; Simon Cooper-Grundy; 'Encyclopaedia of Brighton' by Tim Carder; 'Watch For Me by Moonlight: British Agent With The French Resistance' and 'Mauthausen: History of a Death Camp' by Evelyn Le Chêne.

PART 3

THEY ALSO SERVED

CHAPTER 8

LIEUTENANT ROLAND ALEXANDRE FRENCH SECTION

Photos: TNA

ROLAND ALEXANDRE WAS BORN ON 30 JUNE 1921 IN JOUY-EN JOSAS (78) in south-western Paris. His parents were resident in the Paris suburb of Vincennes, both were French and Alexandre therefore held French nationality. Alexandre was an only child and at some point in his childhood his father, Charles, left the household and his whereabouts thereafter remain unknown. From 1928 to 1937 Alexandre attended the Ecole Saint Jean-Baptiste de la Salle in Paris and gained his *Certificat d'Etudes* there. Alexandre and his mother Marie (née Esnault) relocated to England when in 1936 she married an Englishman, Sidney William Harrild. Though his mother became a British subject, Alexandre retained his French nationality. He completed his secondary education in England from 1937 to 1939 at Shoreham Grammar School (in Pond Road, Shoreham) and when his mother died, Alexandre remained with his stepfather, a hotel manager, in the Brighton area.

Alexandre attended Shoreham Grammar School in Pond Road, Shoreham. The building has since been demolished and Shoreham Community Centre (right) stands on the site. Photos: author's coll.

As war broke out, he was undergoing training in aircraft maintenance and engineering at Brighton's Municipal Technical College (at Richmond Terrace) which involved work experience with what was then known as Phillips and Powis Aircraft, later to be renamed as the Miles Aircraft Limited, at Shoreham Airport. He became fluent in English and on completion of his studies he obtained a job as an aircraft fitter, firstly with Sir Alan Cobham's experimental London Air Park at Hanworth, Middlesex and then with General Aircraft Limited, also at Hanworth, close to the present-day London Heathrow Airport. At that time, General Aircraft had a number of contracts for the British armed forces, including building Hotspur and Hamilcar troop-carrying gliders. While working at Hanworth he lived in Selwyn Avenue, Richmond and became engaged there to a neighbour, Miss Joan Sutton. In mid-1943, despite his vital work on the manufacture of military aircraft Alexandre volunteered for SOE.

Alexandre received his positive vetting from MI5 in early August 1943 and was cleared to join Party 27AC in order to attend STS 7, the Students Assessment Board at Winterfold,

While studying at the Brighton Municipal Technical College in Richmond Terrace, Brighton, Alexandre worked with the Miles aircraft production company at Shoreham Airport. Photo: author's coll.

Cranleigh, Surrey in the latter half of the month. He received a modest 'D' grade ('low but pass') overall, though his intelligence was rated a positive 7/10. His mechanical aptitude was, unsurprisingly, good, but while he was judged to have a 'quick clear mind, courage and perseverance' he was also considered uncertain of himself, hesitant and sometimes indecisive. This, it was thought, could nevertheless be addressed by training and his quiet and pleasing personality made him popular with others. His open, fresh face and slight stature (he was 5'6" tall) made him appear youthful, but Lt-Colonel Charley at Winterfold concluded he would make a good assistant to an organiser.

For his Group A training, Alexandre attended STS 24 at Inverie House, Knoydart in Scotland. Despite his lack of military experience, he was noted to possess a steely enthusiasm for paramilitary training and was glowingly described as self-assured, intelligent, quick-witted, cheerful and adaptable. His conducting officer, Lieutenant Ashley, clearly found Alexandre to be convivial company who, although young in appearance, was serious-minded and applied himself conscientiously and tenaciously to the course, devoting extra study to the subjects in his spare time. Ashley considered him very suitable overall, but particularly as a W/T operator. Ashley also noted, and supported, Alexandre's wish to become a British subject and sympathised with the young man's scant financial means which meant he sometimes struggled to keep up with the spending of some of his fellow students.

No record remains of Alexandre having attended a parachute training course, though he must have gone to RAF Ringway in the latter half of October 1943. From there he went on to his Group B Finishing School at STS 32C at Blackbridge, Beaulieu in November. His reports were again first class, with just one cautionary note that he sometimes worked too quickly, and as a result, inaccurately. Overall, however, he was seen as an agreeable and popular individual, keen to learn and respectful to the training staff.

Rather than being sent for W/T training, Alexandre had been marked out as a potential circuit organiser and as such, he was additionally sent to STS 17 at Brickendonbury Manor, Hertford, for an industrial sabotage course. His report, dated 24 December 1943, showed that his past technical ability had served him well – he was described as an excellent student

Alexandre undertook paramilitary training at STS 24, Inverie House. Photo: author's coll.

who should perform very well in the field. Buoyed by the plaudits of Brickendonbury, Alexandre was confirmed in the role of circuit organiser. He was given a false identity of Roland Eugène Jean Esnault (his late mother's maiden name), with the code name SURVEYOR and the field name *Astre*. He had been commissioned in the General List of the British Army with service number 306148 and his orders were to set up his SURVEYOR circuit in the Poitiers area, based on contacts made there earlier by Major France Antelme (BRICKLAYER/*Antoine*). These were largely railwaymen who were amenable to sabotaging the rail network, engines and rolling stock as an alternative to heavy bombing (and attendant civilian casualties) by the RAF. Alexandre's main contact was to be Adolphe Martin who, following Antelme's return to the UK, had managed to keep his group intact, despite a series of arrests by the Gestapo in the autumn of 1943, and had managed to send a message out via Lisbon saying that he only awaited supplies of arms, material and instructions. Alexandre's job was to find and take over Martin's group and arrange, through radio messages back to England, for drops of arms and supplies.

He was parachuted from a 138 Squadron Halifax (piloted by Flight Lieutenant Thomas) from RAF Tempsford on the night of 8/9 February 1944 in the company of his W/T operator, Lieutenant Robert 'Bud' Byerly (BIOLOGIST/*Gontrand*)and two other French Section agents: Captain François Deniset (MARINER/*Jean-Jacques*) joining the PHONO organisation as arms instructor and Lieutenant Jacques Ledoux (ORATOR/*Homère*), who was to start his own separate circuit. Having been dropped, however, to a reception organised by the Germans using the captured W/T set of Noor Inayat-Khan, all four arriving agents were arrested immediately upon landing.

Alexandre is believed to have first been taken with the three other agents to Fresnes prison on the outskirts of Paris and was later seen by Captain Marcel Rousset, another imprisoned F Section agent who later escaped, at 3 bis Place des Etats Unis in Paris. Rousset was with him and several other captured agents (but not Byerly, Deniset and Ledoux) when, on 18 April 1944, Alexandre was taken via Fresnes prison to the railway station at Vaires-sur-Marne, east of the capital, for deportation. After four days of uncomfortable travel via Maastricht, Düsseldorf, Leipzig, Dresden and Breslau (now Wrocław in Poland) they were

Left to right - Lieutenant Bud Byerly, Captain François Deniset and Lieutenant Jacques Ledoux were all captured with Alexandre as they landed by parachute – victims of the Germans' deadly use of a captured radio link to England; Photos: TNA; Jacqui Pycroft; TNA.

delivered to the fortress prison at Ravitsch, a town historically part of the Kingdom of Prussia in the *Deutsches Kaiserreich*, but ceded to pre-war Poland (and renamed Rawicz) and then re-annexed by Germany early in the Second World War. Conditions in the prison were poor. The agents were kept in solitary confinement and hand-cuffed at night, but were otherwise treated as common criminals – they were made to wear convict clothes and worked at rope making during the day. Alexandre's cell was next door to that of Rousset, who had likewise been transferred to Ravitsch, but who was subsequently returned to Paris and managed to escape while there.

Alexandre was imprisoned after capture at Ravitsch, now Rawicz in Poland. Photo: author.

According to a post-war British Army investigation, it was believed that, in July 1944 after orders were received from Berlin for the execution of the SOE agents at Ravitsch, they were taken in two groups by *SS-Obersturmbannführer* Dr. Wilhelm Scharpwinkel, head of the Breslau Gestapo, from the prison to the KZ Gross-Rosen concentration camp, 100 kilometres to the south west in German Silesia. The camp, together with its 13 sub-camps, held as many as 80,000 inmates and since October 1943 had been under the command of *SS-Sturmbannführer* Johannes Hassebroeck. As special prisoners, the SOE officers transferred from Ravitsch were held in isolation in the *wetterstelle* (weather station) building, slightly apart from the other camp buildings. The first group, believed to total ten, were there only for four or five days when, at dawn on the Sunday morning of either 28 July or 4 August 1944, they were stripped naked and executed by firing squad. The second group, brought shortly afterwards from Ravitsch, were shot immediately after arrival. Witnesses were later to claim that a Ukrainian named Ivan, who worked in the camp's crematorium, extracted gold teeth from four of the victims before their bodies were burned. The discovery in 2011 of Ravitsch prison documentation in Poznan, by Dutch researchers, casts doubt on some of the above British Army findings and instead suggests that British and French SOE agents were transferred to Gross-Rosen on 24 June, 9 July and 4 September 1944.

Alexandre was positively identified, from photographs supplied by SOE, by two prisoners at Gross-Rosen: Kruk-Rostanski, a former Captain in the Polish Army who worked as a clerk in the camp's Manpower Division and Karl Pickel, a German political prisoner. They confirmed that Alexandre had been among the agents executed and Kruk-Rostanski testified that he had been in the first group to be shot.

Alexandre was 23 years old when executed, his body is believed to have been disposed of in the Gross-Rosen crematorium. The Commonwealth War Graves Commission lists his date of death as 19 May 1944, but this probably relates to the last time he was seen alive in the prison at Ravitsch.

Buckmaster's summary of Alexandre, in September 1945 read:

'Extremely unfortunate. Landed to a controlled committee and never had a chance.
A game, competent, plucky, cheerful little man, whom I would be glad to employ.
Would make a most competent organiser. A valuable life.'

A number of former staff who had served at Gross-Rosen at the time of the SOE executions subsequently stood trial for war crimes, all were found guilty. *SS-Obersturmführer* Rudolf-Heinrich Suttrop, adjutant at Gross-Rosen, was put on trial by an American Military Tribunal and hanged in May 1946. The camp's doctor, *SS-Hauptsturmführer* Dr Friedrich-Karl Entress, was similarly tried by an American Military Tribunal for crimes while at Mauthausen-Gusen camp and was hanged in May 1947. In criminal proceeding brought by the Polish authorities in Wrocław in May *SS-Hauptsturmführer* Karl Gallasch was sentenced to be hanged, but cheated his executioner by committing suicide in his cell shortly before his sentence was to be carried out, also in May 1947.

In the trial in 1948 resulting from the British Army's particular investigation of the fate of the SOE agents, former commandant *SS-Sturmbannführer* Johannes Hassebroeck was initially given the death sentence, while *SS-Obersturmführer* Eduardas Drazdauskas (a Lithuanian with responsibility as *Rottenführer* and said to have inflicted beatings and kickings on the SOE prisoners) and *SS-Hauptscharführer* Helmut Eschner, the camp's *Rapportführer*, were sentenced to life imprisonment. Hassebroek had initially been arrested by the Czechoslovakian authorities before being passed to the British for trial. Though sentenced to death, this was quickly commuted to life imprisonment, but he was granted early release in only 1954. He settled in Braunschweig in West Germany where he worked as a sales agent until 1967 when he was arrested under German law for his involvement in the camps. He was accused of being personally responsible for the killings of nine Jews and three other inmates at Gross-Rosen, but was acquitted firstly by the Braunschweig court and then again, following an appeal by the prosecution, by the Federal Constitutional Court of Germany. He continued to be under investigation until his death in 1977. Other Gross-Rosen staff implicated in the executions were *SS-Untersharf*ührer Frinke, reported to have been killed in action in the later stages of the war, and *SS-Obersturmführer* Walter Ernstberger, the *Schutzhaftlager*führer responsible for day-to-day operation of the camp, who was believed to have committed suicide in 1945. *SS-Obersturmbannführe*r Wilhelm Scharpwinkel, head of the Breslau Gestapo, was reported to have died in a Russian prison in 1948. Before his death, British investigators had named him as wanted for his involvement in the execution of several of the 50 murdered recaptured escapees of 'The Great Escape' of Allied officers from Stalag Luft III in April 1944.

Above left - Johannes Hassebroek, camp commandant at Gross-Rosen, whose death sentence was comuted to imprisonment. Above right – seen awaiting his post-war trial, Rudolf-Heinrich Suttrop, the camp's adjutant who was executed in 1946. Photos – author's coll. and USHMM.

Alexandre did not receive any award due to his having been captured immediately on arrival in France. Along with many other SOE agents with no known grave, he is officially commemorated on the Commonwealth War Graves Commission's Brookwood Memorial, near Woking, Surrey – panel 21, column 3 and is listed on the SOE Memorial at Valençay, France. His name heads the list of 19 executed F Section agents on the SOE memorial at the site of the former Gross-Rosen concentration camp near Rogoźnica, Poland. The memorial's granite came from the camp's quarry where many prisoners had been forced to work.

Alexandre is commemorated on the memorial to the 19 executed F Section agents at the site of the Gross-Rosen concentration camp near Rogoźnica, Poland. Photo - author.

The cremator (left) and entrance gate (right), on the present-day site of KZ Gross-Rosen. Photos - author.

Alexandre's name on the Brookwood Memorial. Photos: Holly McCue.

Sources and acknowledgements: Alexandre's SOE personal file is (TNA) HS9/21/4. The investigation into war crimes at Gross-Rosen is (TNA) WO 311/532.

Chapter 9

LIEUTENANT FRANK BEC
LÉGION D'HONNEUR
FRENCH SECTION

Photos: TNA

FRANCISQUE EUGÈNE BEC, KNOWN AS 'FRANK', WAS BORN 18 OCTOBER 1905 in Palmers Green, north London. He was one of the family of three sons and one daughter of French parents, Antoine Francisque Bec and Katherine 'Katie' Bec (née La Brousse), who had homes in Ruislip, Middlesex and in Grenoble in France. Bec had dual British/French nationality and is recorded as having attended primary and junior school in England - in Matlock, Derbyshire and Brighton, Sussex, though no further details have yet been found. For his secondary education he went to France and was at school in Boulogne, followed by trade education and training in Grenoble.

Bec chose to serve his national military service in France and was consequently in the French Air Force from 1925 to 1927. He worked in a semi-military capacity in French aviation for a further year in 1928, but then returned to Britain and from 1929 to 1939 worked in leather and soft goods, firstly in his father's business specialising in gloves, gaiters and berets, based in Cheapside, London EC2 and then as a merchant/manufacturer's agent in Noble Street, also in London EC2. He was married, and although his Swedish wife (Karin Elisabet, née Ekelund, originally from Stockholm) and daughter Yvonne, born in 1935, had moved to Sweden just before war broke out in 1939, they were still in frequent contact with Bec.

Bec in earlier life.
Photos: Martin Paul Hobbs.

With his wife and child safely in Sweden, Bec returned to France in 1940 and joined the French Army, serving in a liaison capacity with the British Army's Royal Army Service Corps (RASC). He was demobilised in July 1940 at Toulouse and then worked at several jobs in the unoccupied zone in Grenoble. In September 1942 he crossed to Spain and subsequently reached Britain. He was held at MI5's interrogation centre at the Royal Victoria Patriotic School, Wandsworth, south-west London, while the authorities assured themselves of the details of his escape from France via Spain – this being a necessary process in order to identify any enemy 'plants' entering the country. In Bec's case, this was not straightforward and was to cast something of a shadow on his early SOE career during training. His memory and details proved poor during MI5's questioning and at times he could not explain facts easily. While his interrogator concluded that he was nevertheless being truthful, MI5 provided a less than glowing report on Bec, but it was adequate for him then to join the RASC of the British Army in the rank of Private. His two brothers also took an active part in the war effort, one served as an officer at Free French Headquarters in Stafford Place, London, the other in the British Army at the REME workshops in Malta.

Bec volunteered for SOE in June 1943, but did not undergo his initial assessment until February 1944. This delay may have been as a result of his MI5 report, dated July 1943, which detailed his interrogator's dissatisfaction with Bec's telling of the story of his escape from France and Spain. After this hiatus, however, Bec was accepted in February 1944 to go forward to the Students Assessment Board (SAB) at STS 7, Winterfold, Cranleigh, Surrey.

If anyone looked less like the secret agent of popular imagination, it was probably Bec. Of medium height, with prematurely thinning hair, a pale face, stocky build and brusque manner of speech, he appeared older than his years and was somewhat of a loner who was inclined to keep himself to himself, showed no sense of humour, and found it difficult to socialise. One description of him mentions a 'loose gait', a legacy perhaps of his over-large size 12 feet, combined with having one shoulder two inches lower than the other - requiring padding in his uniform and clothing. He commenced SAB on 17 February 1944 and his report, dated 20 February 1944, recorded an overall D rating (Low, but pass) and described him as 'a sincere, reserved, serious-minded person' who, while 'lacking in dominance' and being perceived to have 'a certain amount of mental confusion', was nevertheless praised for 'a quiet, steady, methodical manner' and for being 'wholly reliable'.

From Winterfold, Bec went on to his paramilitary Group A training at STS 24A, Inverie House, Knoydart, near Mallaig in Scotland. Lieutenant Goddard, conducting officer throughout Bec's paramilitary and parachute training, characterised Bec as someone who might be taken for a dour, taciturn, north country Englishman on first acquaintance, with a reserved nature which led him to generally work independently of his fellow trainees. Under the surface, however, his outlook and his sympathies were judged to incline towards France. Though calm, self-controlled, painstaking and conscientious, his efforts were spoiled by mistakes and he was rated very slow and 'wool-gathering' by Goddard. Despite this, Bec was seen as one of the steadiest members of his group and was passed to progress to his parachute course at STS 51, RAF Ringway, his course commencing on 20 March 1944. It was noted that Bec was not enthusiastic about the training, but typically stoic, he worked hard, though a little nervously, during the ground instruction. He successfully completed four descents, but was only rated Second Class as he had a habit of throwing up his hands on jumping, thereby making his exits from the aircraft 'ragged'.

For his Group B Finishing School course at Beaulieu, Bec was sent to STS 32C, Blackbridge, starting on 9 April 1944 and he successfully completed the training with the recommendation that he was suitable to become an assistant circuit organiser. He was therefore finally sent to a Group C Operational School, STS 40 at Howbury Hall, near Bedford, where he achieved satisfactory and good reports in the organisation of reception committees and operation of the S-phone and Eureka equipment. A cautionary note added that he needed much more practice.

With no time available for more practice, Bec was sent as Technical Instructor (responsible for weapons instruction in particular) to Sydney Hudson's HEADMASTER circuit, working in the Le Mans area. His false identity was Francisque Eugène Labrousse, (though once in the field he had a second false identity of Raymond Perrin), his code name was BORER and his field name was *Hugues*. In the company of two other agents, Sonia Butt and Raymond Glaesner, Bec parachuted into France on the night of 28/29 May 1944 from a B-24 Liberator of the USAAF from RAF Harrington, piloted by Lieutenant Emanuel Choper. The drop zone was at Le Clos, 1 kilometre south of La Cropte and 32 kilometres south-east of Laval (Mayenne), but on arrival, his accent caused so much concern, despite his SAB report having credited him with 'perfect English and French', that it was agreed that he would therefore join a *Maquis* camp in the countryside, training the French in sabotage and weapons use.

The crew of the USAAF B-24 Liberator, piloted by Lieutenant Choper (second left, front row) that dropped Bec on 28/29 May 1944. Photo: Tom Ensminger coll.

Bec was to serve as an instructor for the Maquis in the HEADMASTER circuit of Sydney Hudson, pictured. Photo: author's coll.

Bec's commission as a Second Lieutenant in the General List, with service number 322014, was only confirmed with effect from 5 June 1944, after his despatch to France, but would have helped his standing among the Etival *Maquis*, to whose camp he was attached in the Forêt de Charnie (72) Sarthe, near to the Abbaye d'Étival. It was there, only three weeks after his arrival, that an enemy force, reported to consist of up to 120 Germans and 80 *Milice*, attacked the camp. The 27 *maquisards*, faced with overwhelming odds, had little option other than to flee, but Bec, together with Claude Hilleret, one of the *maquisards*, stayed behind to provide covering fire with their Sten guns. Seven Germans and two Milice were accounted for, but both Bec and Hilleret were shot and killed. Bec's SOE file quotes a date of 11 August 1944 for the action, later corrected to 16 June 1944, the latter then being quoted in the Commonwealth War Graves Commission's records. Local French historians of the Sarthe *Résistance* are certain, however, that the enemy's attack, the result of a betrayal, and Bec's death, occurred on the evening of 20 June 1944. He and Hilleret were buried with full military honours following a joint funeral ceremony, attended by hundreds of local people.

Bec was aged 38 at the time of his death, he lies in a formal British military grave in the 1939-45 section of Le Mans West Cemetery, Plot 38, Row C, Grave 50. A quiet, unpretentious, but brave man, Bec was awarded a posthumous Mention in Despatches by the British and was made a *Chevalier de la Légion d'Honneur* by the French. He is commemorated at the French Section Memorial at Valençay; signs in the Forêt de Charnie mark the 1944 position of the *Maquis* camp and a cairn near Etival en Charnie commemorated where Bec and Hilleret fell, but has since been moved to a nearby road where it is more accessible. Both men are also remembered on the *Monument aux Morts* in the nearby village of Chemiré en Charnie.

Bec's wife and daughter returned to England after the war and Karin remarried in 1968, becoming Mrs Bradshaw.

Sources and acknowledgements: Bec's SOE personal file is (TNA) HS9 111/5, though it has scant content. His circuit organiser, Sydney Hudson, in his biography, 'Undercover Operator', mentions Bec, but further confuses his date of death. Family details and photographs were provided by Martin Paul Hobbs, nephew of Frank Bec and Jacquie Ashcroft, a niece.

The funeral and burial of Bec, together with Claude Hilleret. Photos: Martin Paul Hobbs

Bec's grave in Le Mans West cemetery. Photo: author.

The cairn in the Forêt de Charnie commemorating Bec and Claude Hilleret. Photo: Paul-Martin Hobbs.

Chapter 10

LIEUTENANT MARCUS BLOOM
FRENCH SECTION

Photos: TNA and Martin
Sugarman

MARCUS REGINALD BLOOM WAS BORN IN SHOREDITCH, IN THE EAST END of London, on 24 September 1907, the second of the four sons of Harry Bloom and his wife Anna (née Davidoff). The Blooms were a Jewish family, with roots in Poland for Harry, though born in England, and in Russia for Anna, born in Germany before being brought to England. Both their families lived in the Jewish community in the East End where Harry and Anna met and married. They initially lived in Brick Lane, but after Marcus was born they moved to Tottenham. During the First World War the family again moved, to Hove in Sussex and it was while there that Marcus went to Hove High School at 49 Clarendon Villas.

Bloom went to school at Hove High School which was then at 49 Clarendon Villas, Hove. Photo: Malcolm, Conor and Lucas Hatch.

Bloom's father was a businessman whose commercial interests included a restaurant in Hove and the Super Palace cinema in Battersea, south-west London. After completing his education, Bloom helped his father with management of the restaurant in Hove, the cinema and another developing family business, a mail order textile firm, Sterling Textiles. In 1931, Bloom's father chose Marcus to go to Paris to manage the French interests of Sterling Textiles, the business fared well and Bloom began to mix with several wealthy and aristocratic Parisians, developing interests in riding, horse racing, polo, and shooting. He met a young woman, Germaine Berthe Fevrier who, sharing some of his new interests, was keen on shooting and frequently attended horse racing meetings with Bloom.

After seven successful years, however, Sterling Textiles suffered as a result of a newspaper campaign in Britain against mail order businesses and Bloom returned to England in 1937. In March 1938 he married Germaine in London, but his new wife could not settle in the apartment they took in Cricklewood, London NW2 and frequently returned to France where her widowed mother still lived in the family home at Barneville-sur-Mer on the Channel coast in Normandy.

One of Bloom's passions and business ventures was the cinema, he managed the Super Palace venue in York Road, Battersea SW11. Photo: author's coll.

Germaine was stranded in France when the country capitulated in 1940, while in England Bloom was increasingly frustrated by his lack of luck in immediately volunteering for military service. He had gone to the Army recruiting centre closest to his father's cinema in Battersea and had told the recruiting sergeant of his fluency in French and his wish to use it in the service of his country. But although he was called for an interview at the War Office, his French was not tested and he was told he could not be used in any specialist capacity because his mother had been born in Germany. Only temporarily thwarted, he instead volunteered for the Royal Artillery and joined the colours in the ranks as a Gunner (Private) in January 1941, with the service number 1113627. He was first sent to the Royal Artillery's Signals Training Regiment, but his education, intelligence and maturity soon showed him to be a potential officer and he was then sent in November 1941 to 124 Officer Cadet

Training Unit (OCTU) in Llandrindod Wells, Wales for training as a gunnery officer for an anti-aircraft unit.

His training was due to complete in April 1942, but Bloom's patience did not last that long and his application for special duties involving his command of French at last succeeded when he was granted an interview with Captain Maufe of French Section, SOE in early February 1942. Just over two weeks later he was interviewed a second time in Room O55A at the former Victoria Hotel in Northumberland Avenue. His interviewer (noted as 'LG' and therefore probably Major Lewis Gielgud, brother of the already-famous actor John Gielgud) used the term 'Pink Jew' to describe Bloom, in a manner all too prevalent at the time, but went on to add 'keen, and I liked him'.

As a result of this summary, Bloom was cleared by MI5 on 27 February 1942 and was taken on strength by F Section on 16 March 1942. To protect his wife still in France he was given the name of Michel Blount during his training, the first preliminary school element of which was at STS 5, Wanborough Manor. Bloom was a member of Party 27N which went there in early April 1942; his reports were generally good, with the exception of fieldcraft where he was judged to have no natural instinct for the work. His build was also considered to count against him, in his physical training he was described as carrying a lot of weight, not being fit and not improving much. His interest in shooting as a pastime nevertheless served him well in weapons training where he did well and was noted to be a good shot. Thanks to his previous signaling experience in the Royal Artillery, he scored the maximum in signaling and communications and overall was rated by Lieutenant Turner as 'steady' and 'rather a humorist and given to showing off a little'. Turner also made reference to Bloom's Jewishness, describing him as 'slightly Jewish in his outlook and appearance'. This continuing emphasis on his race was then sadly taken to an extreme by the normally urbane and charming Colonel de Wesselow, commandant at Wanborough Manor, who would seem to have taken against Bloom. In his self-contradictory summary, de Wesselow viciously commented:

'mental and physical effort seems to come hard to this pink yid. In conversation, at least with myself, he is dull-minded and by no means forthcoming; though not an oyster, maybe he keeps under the shell the usual racial nimbleness'.

Despite this narrow-minded racial stereotyping, de Wesselow also noted, to the contrary, that Bloom was:

'certainly observant and intelligent and on one scheme produced as good a report as one could want. Enjoys the weapons training and takes his W/T seriously'.

Clearly unable to make up his mind, or perhaps to overcome his prejudices, de Wesselow concluded that Bloom 'may or may not be genuine and sincere'.

To his credit, Bloom was able to lay to rest de Wesselow's more disparaging comments during the remainder of his training. From Wanborough Manor he continued with Party

27N for paramilitary training in Scotland and shone at STS 23, Meoble Lodge, Morar, Inverness-shire. Even in physical training it was noted, by the middle of May 1942, that his improvement had been remarkable. His build was again acknowledged not to help (his rope climbing suffered in particular) and though his fieldwork had improved to 'average' it was noted, perhaps also due to his somewhat rotund build, that he was 'too fond of skylines'. His schemes and tactics continued to draw high praise and Major Watts, as officer commanding STS 23, gave Bloom a glowing report, saying he had:

'…done very well indeed. His willingness to try anything has been an excellent example to the others. Possessed of a keen sense of humour, he has been the life and soul of the party, is a very nice fellow who has plenty of intelligence and 'guts'. Company seems to stimulate him to greater efforts, so he should work very well with others. Seems very English'.

Now firmly set on the path to becoming an agent, Bloom received his commission on 26 May 1942. Contrary to a note on his SOE file that he was transferred to the Intelligence Corps, Second Lieutenant Bloom became an officer in the British Army's General List, with the new service number 236314.

There is no record of Bloom attending parachute training school, though other members of Party 27N did so. But with his role as a W/T Operator confirmed, he then went on, in early June 1942 to STS 52 at Thame Park, Oxfordshire, where he undertook the full W/T course, before attending a Finishing School at Beaulieu. Again, no record remains of which school he went to, but the other W/T operator members of Party 27N attended STS 32a, Hartford House. A report survives on his SOE file of the scheme he undertook in Loughborough, he did extremely well on this and his report summary dated 22 August 1942 reads:

'This student is security minded and most discreet, both in his conversation and his habits. He had taken great pains to conceal his set and his papers. He always kept the door of his room locked.'

After a spell of leave at home, Bloom returned to French Section to receive his orders. He was allocated as W/T operator to the PIMENTO circuit already established by Captain Tony Brooks (PIMENTO/*Alphonse*) in and around Toulouse. Bloom's codename was BISHOP, his field name *Urbain* and his false identity in the name of Michel Boileau. For whatever reason (most likely because he had not completed a parachute course) it was decided that Bloom was to be sent to France by sea, landing on the French southern coast.

The first step along that route was for him to be shipped to Gibraltar, a voyage that he undertook in mid-October 1942 and once there he was taken into the charge of SOE's naval operations section. According to official records (Bloom's family believed that he was delivered to France by submarine from Gibraltar, but Odette Sansom clearly recalled Bloom being with her) he was then among a group of agents put aboard the felucca *Seadog*, captained by Lieutenant Jan Buchowski. On the night of 3/4 November, the *Seadog* hove to off the French coast in the secluded *calanque*, or cove, of Port-Miou, some three kilometres south-west of Cassis (13). At least eight agents were landed, among them Bloom and fellow French Section colleagues George Starr (WHEELWRIGHT/*Hilaire*), Mary Herbert (JEWELLER/*Claudine*), Marie-Thérèse Le Chêne (WISTERIA/*Adèle*) and Odette Sansom (CLOTHIER/*Lise*). A smaller party was brought out of France in *Seadog's* dinghy, including the French Section agents John Starr (ACROBAT/*Bob*), the brother of the incoming George Starr, and Isidore Newman (DIVIDEND/*Julien*).

Bloom was put ashore in the cove at Port-Miou on the south coast of France. Photo: author's coll.

Bloom's orders were to make his way to Toulouse and contact Brooks, who worked in a warehouse. This he did, but according to Professor Michael Foot in the official history of French Section, Bloom immediately committed two security breaches. Firstly, he revealed that he had spent his first 24 hours in Toulouse seeking out his fellow French Section agent, Maurice Pertschuk (PRUNUS/*Eugène*). The two Jewish agents had become friends during training and had secretly agreed a social rendez-vous in Toulouse before Bloom was due to make contact with Brooks. The latter, according to Professor Foot (and probably based on personal information from Brooks himself) was doubly angered when Bloom arrived at the warehouse rendez-vous and greeted him cheerily in English. Before he could prove his worth, Bloom was therefore damned in the opinion of his circuit leader and Brooks declared he would have nothing to do with him. Bloom was consequently passed on to Pertschuk, to whom (despite their age differences – Pertschuk was then just 21, while Bloom was 35) Bloom was more than happy to report and serve. Brooks, meantime, continued to rely on sending his messages via courier to Switzerland, for transmission from the British Embassy in Berne to London.

After his arrival in France, Bloom transferred to act as W/T operator to the PRUNUS circuit of his friend, Maurice Pertschuk. Photo: Anne Whiteside.

In the event, Pertschuk initially benefitted little from Bloom's arrival, since the latter was unable to transmit on his W/T set due to an apparent technical problem. Nevertheless eager to participate, Bloom started work with Pertschuk by making contacts among the postal workers in Toulouse and helping to reconnoiter potential sabotage targets, in particular the huge powder factory in Toulouse that was now working on production for the Germans. He was also credited with having helped with the destruction of an enemy train in January 1943.

It was not that same month that Adolphe Rabinovitch (CATALPHA/*Arnaud*), another F Section W/T operator, arrived in Toulouse to see if he might repair Bloom's W/T set. When he tried it, however, it worked first time and, undoubtedly to Bloom's embarrassment, Rabinovitch announced that the problem simply lay in Bloom having tried to use too long an antenna. Fortunately, Rabinovitch had experienced the same problem when he had first tried to transmit from France. When he later reported on solving Bloom's issue, he was therefore not critical of Bloom (whom, on the contrary, he described as courageous and very willing), but of the limited amount of technical instruction that trainee agents were given in England.

Bloom now began to carry out his primary role of W/T operator, sending and receiving over 50 messages for PRUNUS and also helping with sending messages for George Starr's WHEELWRIGHT circuit. He continued to work as a lieutenant to Pertschuk, organising the reception of four drops of weapons and explosives for the PRUNUS circuit and taking part in sabotage operations himself. The circuit was established throughout the Haute-Garonne region, around Toulouse, Montréjeu and Fonsorbes. Close to the latter village,

Bloom was provided with a safe house and base for his W/T transmissions by Count Jean d'Aligny who put his country house at Esquiré at the disposal of PRUNUS. Helped by his partner, Yvonne Lagrange, d'Aligny had already hidden some 35 tons of French Army military supplies on his estate. The nucleus of helpers at d'Aligny's house included a Doctor Jacobsen; a Spaniard, Robert Cunillera; and a young woman Jeanine Messerli (also recorded as Jeanine Morisse) who particularly helped Bloom by acting as his courier to and from Pertschuk.

The downfall of PRUNUS began on 12 April 1943 with the arrest of Pertschuk and his girlfriend, Madame Odette Larocque, who had acted as a courier and letter box for the circuit. The following night, a raid by the Germans on d'Aligny's house netted Bloom, Cunillera, Yvonne Lagrange and Jean d'Aligny. Bloom later told the story of his arrest to a fellow prisoner at Fresnes, a Parisian named Colle. Bloom had been handcuffed to Cunillera, but at the British agent's prompting, they leapt from a window and managed to escape into the night-time cover of the countryside. They crossed a river seven times in case their pursuers used tracker dogs, but when Cunillera became too exhausted to continue, the Spaniard suggested they make for the *Gendarmerie* in Muret, only some 12 kilometres from their starting point. They reached the police station at 5 a.m., but instead of being able to talk to a pro-*Résistance* captain whom Cunillera knew, they were received by a *Brigadier* (Lance-Corporal). The latter promised to fetch the captain, but instead the Gestapo were informed and soon arrived to re-arrest the two fugitives.

Bloom was arrested at the country house. Esquiré, of Count Jean d'Aligny. Photo: Janny Bonnet.

From Muret, Bloom was taken to the Gestapo headquarters in the rue Maignac (now the rue des Martyrs de la Libération) in Toulouse. He was seen on his way there, as later reported by Rabinovitch, being led through the streets with a bloodied face. He was then sent to Fresnes prison, on the outskirts of Paris, where he shared a cell with Colle, as already described, and where he was seen by another French Section agent, Marcel Rousset. A local recruit to PRUNUS who was also captured, Marcel Petit, was fortunate (like Jean d'Aligny) to return from deportation and stated that the Germans had a photograph of Pertschuk in British Army uniform. It was believed that the photograph had been taken to France by Bloom, (though any purpose in his having done so is questionable) in yet another breach of security. This, coupled with reports of the members of PRUNUS displaying scant caution by dining together and even talking English, has unfortunately cast a shadow over the achievements of Bloom (and Pertschuk) in the PRUNUS circuit.

Bloom was badly beaten after capture and was held at the Gestapo headquarters in Toulouse. Photo: Janny Bonnet.

Having captured Bloom's radio set, the Germans made immediate attempts to continue transmitting to London. Josef Goetz, the SD's *funkspiel* expert in Paris, attempted to imitate Bloom's W/T traffic, but London was suspicious. A message was sent by SOE to which Bloom would have known the answer, Goetz could only attempt or guess a reply, and it was then clear that Bloom's set was controlled by the enemy.

The next that was heard of Bloom came in July 1943 when Auguste Floiras (SADDLER/ *Albert*) reported that Bloom was believed to have been executed in Fresnes prison. This rumour was repeated two weeks later by George Starr (WHEELWRIGHT/*Hilaire*) who stated that he had been given this information by an Inspector in the *Sûreté*, though the latter had not been a witness. This story was disproved however, when information was received that Bloom was still being held in Fresnes and details of his initial escape and subsequent recapture were given when another agent reached England and was debriefed. Marcel Rousset was later to confirm that while imprisoned in Fresnes, he had seen Bloom, whom he had met while undergoing radio training at Thame Park. German records show that they had full details of Bloom, including his code and field names, his date of birth and his civilian occupation as a cinema operator.

A French railway worker, Léopold Turcan, also shared a cell with Bloom in Fresnes and later gave the family a description of how Bloom was taken for questioning at the avenue Foch on at least two occasions. Each time Bloom returned to Fresnes he described how he had been badly beaten, but he maintained he had given nothing away. He was able to get news of his imprisonment to his wife, Germaine, who moved to Paris and arranged for food parcels to be smuggled in to her husband. The British authorities later reimbursed her for the 50,000 francs she had spent in this activity.

From the post-war investigation by Vera Atkins into the fate of missing French Section agents, it was suggested that Bloom had been moved from Fresnes in May 1944. He is believed to have firstly been sent to the Ravitsch high-security prison, but then transferred at the end of August 1944 to Mauthausen concentration camp in Austria. The camp's records show the arrival of 47 Allied prisoners on 1 September 1944: 39 Dutch, 7 British and one American. They were held under close guard as a group in the camp's transport depot until, after only a few days, each had a number painted on his chest - representing the order in which they were to be shot the next day.

On 6 September 1944 the prisoners were taken in two groups, one in the morning and one in the afternoon, from the depot building and marched, under guard, down a 180-step stone staircase into the camp's quarry where more armed SS waited for them. Other inmates who survived the camp were able to witness and later report the grim farce then carried out by the Germans. For whatever reason, it seems that the camp's authorities had decided on a charade that the prisoners would be shot 'while trying to escape'. Consequently at least some of the prisoners were ordered to run back up the stone steps and were gunned down as they did so. Yugoslav prisoners who were present later told one of Bloom's brothers, Bernard, that Marcus had thrown a rock at a guard, knocking him down the steps, and had then made a dash for it up the staircase before he, too, was machine-gunned. Among the 47 executed were five fellow French Section agents, Georges Clement, Sidney Jones, Isidore Newman, Edward Wilkinson and John Young.

Colonel Buckmaster's summary evaluation of Bloom's service read:

'The risk of sending to the Field this officer with his imperfect French and his Anglo-Saxon-Jewish appearance was only justified by our extreme penury in W/TO's. He was very courageous in the Field and fought to a finish. The details of his arrest are still obscure, but it is clear that he did a good job for many months.'

The stone steps leading from the quarry at Mauthausen where Bloom met his death. Photo: author.

From the British, Bloom received a posthumous Mention in Despatches; the French authorities gave no award.

Proceedings against 61 former officials at Mauthausen began on 29 March 1946 and ended on 13 May 1946. The main trial was followed by other subsidiary trials. The charges brought before a US military court against the defendants covered a range of crimes throughout the camp's existence, but included the testimony of inmates that 46-49 Dutch and British intelligence agents had been sent to Mauthausen in early September 1944 and wearing only underwear, shirts and no shoes were escorted under guard into the quarry (commonly known as the *Wiener Graben* – the Vienna Ditch), around 300 metres from the camp's main entrance. Some two thirds were shot in the morning, and the remainder in the afternoon.

A high proportion of the accused, 49 of the 61, were executed, reflecting judgment on the brutality at the camp. SS-Standartenführer Franz Ziereis, camp commandant, was never brought before a Military Tribunal. He died at the Mauthausen camp, where he was brought on 23 May 1945 after he was shot and seriously wounded by an American soldier 'while attempting to escape' from his hunting lodge on the Pyhrn mountain, 100 kilometres to the south. He died soon after arrival in the camp.

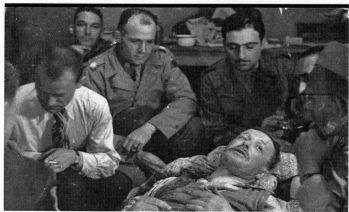

Above: Ziereis (centre) with two staff at KZ-Mauthausen; and (left) on his death bed after being shot by an American soldier. Photos – author's coll.

Bloom is officially commemorated on the Brookwood Memorial near Woking, Surrey, panel 21, column 3. In addition to his listing at the Valençay memorial, he is also remembered on the roll of honour at the St. John's Wood Synagogue, London NW8 and on a plaque on his mother's grave (block X, row 10) in the Edmonton Federation Synagogue cemetery in London N9. At the site of KZ-Mauthausen, Bloom is remembered on a plaque to the 47 murdered agents and on a private memorial erected by his family.

Sources and acknowledgements: Bloom's SOE personal file is at TNA HS9/166/7. 'Lieutenant Marcus Bloom: a Jewish hero of the SOE', by Martin Sugarman was published in 2004 in volume 39 of Jewish Historical Studies. Martin Sugarman kindly permitted use of that material, which included details from the Bloom family. Additional material from the Toulouse and Fonsorbes area was provided by Madame Janny Bonnet.

The memorial at the site of KZ-Mauthausen to the Allied agents executed there, Bloom's name is unfortunately mis-spelled. Photo: author.

CHAPTER 11

CHARLES FRASER-SMITH
MINISTRY OF SUPPLY

Photo: author's coll.

CHARLES FRASER-SMITH, CONSIDERED TO HAVE BEEN THE INSPIRATION

for the character 'Q' in the James Bond books and films, was born on 26 January 1904, the son of a solicitor, Edward James Fraser-Smith, who also owned a wholesale grocery business. He was orphaned at the age of seven and then brought up, together with his three siblings, by an aunt and uncle, both strongly-committed Christians, in Croxley Green, Hertfordshire. He attended Watford Grammar School and then Brighton College where he was described as 'scholastically useless except for woodwork and science and making things.' The latter abilities were nevertheless to be the attributes that brought Fraser-Smith to the public eye in the later stages of a peripatetic and adventurous life.

On leaving Brighton College at the age of 17, Fraser-Smith first took a one-year position as a teacher of sports and elementary science at a preparatory school in Portsmouth. When the job finished, he flirted with the idea of studying medicine or engineering before settling on a three-year farming course and apprenticeship in Littlehampton.

A holiday to Morocco inspired Fraser-Smith with the Christian missionary zeal of his adoptive parents and he returned to finish his farming studies, determined to undertake missionary farming in north Africa. Before departing, he went to Paris to study French intensively, appreciating that he would need a good command of the language and he then left for Morocco in 1926. He was to stay there some 14 years, setting up a missionary farm as well as managing farms for the King of Morocco and its Chief Religious Judge. In 1930 he married another missionary worker, Blanche Ellis, whom he had met in Paris and was then working in Casablanca. A family was started with the birth of a son, Brian, and Fraser-Smith and his wife diversified from farming when they accepted a plea to take over the management of one orphanage, and then established another.

As the Vichy French government's grip tightened on Morocco, the Fraser-Smith family returned to England in 1940. Charles first took a job as a despatch rider for Civil Defence in London before moving the family to Headingley, Leeds in Yorkshire where his wife's family lived. He signed on as a worker at the Avro aircraft factory in nearby Yeadon, but had not been there long when he delivered a talk on his Moroccan work and adventures at the Open Brethren Evangelical Church in Leeds, detailing the necessity of procuring supplies from any source available. His ability to do so, evidenced by his successes in Morocco, impressed two senior officials of Britain's Ministry of Supply who, by chance, were among the congregation. One of them was the Director of the Ministry of Supply on a visit from London and he and his Leeds-based representative were both convinced that Fraser-Smith would have the necessary flexibility and ingenuity that wartime called for, with the ability to procure supplies by means that would not be contemplated by existing and bureaucratic civil servants. As a result, the Director offered him what Fraser-Smith later described as "a funny job in London".

For a brief period he was based in the Ministry's Leeds office and while there an early challenge was to procure counterfeit Spanish Army uniforms for a proposed plan by then newly-formed SOE to infiltrate agents into Spain should the Spanish decide to enter the war on the side of Germany. Fraser-Smith dealt directly with local textile suppliers and fulfilled the order.

After this initial flurry of activity, Fraser-Smith moved back to his original family home in Croxley Green, Hertfordshire and began the daily train commute to his Ministry of Supply office in Portland House, Tothill Street, London SW1. Officially, Fraser-Smith was a temporary civil servant for the Ministry's Clothing and Textile Department (Dept. CT6). His job, however, was largely responsible to the Secret Intelligence Service (SIS/MI6), operating from its headquarters at Minimax House, 54 Broadway, for the supply and development of specialised equipment for the intelligence services and special forces operating in occupied Europe. In addition to SIS/MI6, he worked for SOE, Naval Intelligence, MI5 and MI9. For the latter organization he invented numerous gadgets intended to help prisoners of war to escape and evaders, such as shot-down airmen, to get back to Britain. His aptitude and his interest in gadgetry led him to develop a wide range of devices, including miniature cameras inside cigarette lighters; shaving brushes that could contain rolled-up film; hairbrushes that could conceal a map and a saw; steel shoelaces that doubled as a garrote or gigli saw; an asbestos-lined pipe for carrying secret documents, and pens that contained compasses. As an example of his ability to think laterally, Fraser-Smith used a special left-hand thread for the disguised screw-off top of a hidden-document container, suggesting that this would prevent discovery by the "unswerving logic of the German mind", as no German would ever think of trying to unscrew something the wrong way. Later in the war Fraser-Smith also supplied the Special Air Service (SAS) and the forerunner to America's CIA, the Office of Strategic Services (OSS), who liaised closely with, in particular, Britain's SOE.

Fraser-Smith called his inventions 'Q gadgets' after the 'Q ships' of the First World War that saw apparently-unarmed merchant freighters, carrying cleverly-concealed heavy armament , lure enemy submarines into surface attacks. But while Fraser-Smith's later fame flowed from such gadgets, he estimated that only 10% of his work involved his own developments, while 50% of the orders he received were to exact specifications and 40% were to approximate specifications and it was his expertise in supply that was therefore more crucial. One such success in supply was to be recorded in SOE's annals of inventive action against the enemy and involved a unique form of sabotage in 1943. One of the most successful agents of SOE's French Section was Captain Ben Cowburn, codenamed TINKER and with the field name *Germain*. His TINKER circuit was particularly well-established in the city of Troyes in France where a local helper called Pierre Mulsant had become one of Cowburn's most-trusted supporters. In turn, one of Mulsant's most dedicated and willing helpers, largely as a courier, was a vivacious young woman, Yvonne Fontaine, known as *Nenette*. Already twice divorced, Fontaine worked for the laundry business of Monsieur Naraud in Troyes who, although a sympathiser of the *Résistance*, nevertheless performed laundry work for the enemy authorities. When he won a large contract with the German army to dye linen underwear into a more military green, not only did he short-change the Germans in terms of quantities delivered, but he also added itching powder, supplied to SOE by Fraser-Smith, into the finished garments. Monsieur Hubert Herbin, a director of *Usine Herbin* in Troyes, performed a similar service in impregnating shirts and singlets which he was producing for German submarine crews. The itching powder developed for SOE was no common joke itching powder, but made so strong that exposure could be excruciating. It was claimed that some 25,000 uniform items of clothing were contaminated with the powder, with *Kriegsmarine* U-boat crews being most affected. A story, though unsubstantiated, even went around the *Résistance* in Troyes that one enemy submarine had to turn round and return to base when its crew became afflicted with severe itching. Both Pierre Mulsant and Yvonne Fontaine performed so well in occupied France that they were flown out to be trained as fully-fledged agents. While both subsequently returned to France (Mulsant as MINISTER/*Paul* and Fontaine as FLORIST/*Mimi*) and continued to serve with distinction, Mulsant was arrested with his British radio operator in July 1944 and executed in October 1944 at Buchenwald concentration camp. Yvonne Fontaine survived the war.

Pierre Mulsant was the agent of French Section SOE who arranged for Fraser-Smith's itching powder to be added to clothing made for the German armed forces, including (right) U-boat crews. Photos: TNA and author's coll.

Fraser-Smith was also involved in the intelligence operation codenamed OPERATION MINCEMEAT, which was designed to drop a body off the coast of Spain in April 1943, carrying false papers to mislead the Germans regarding the planning for an invasion of Italy. He was ordered to design a container 6' 2" long and 3' wide, to carry a 'deadweight' of 200 lb that would be preserved in dry ice. When the dry ice evaporated, it filled the canister with carbon dioxide and drove out any oxygen, thus preserving the body without refrigeration. The successful operation was the basis of the book and later film '*The Man Who Never Was*'.

After the war, Fraser-Smith continued working for the Ministry of Supply until 1947. A period of ill-health prevented a return to Morocco, but in 1948 he bought a rundown dairy farm at Burrington in Devon and, using his previous experience in north Africa, coupled with his flair for practical and technological solutions, turned it into a profitable business. In the late 1970s, his family persuaded him to seek permission to write a book about his wartime exploits. With clearance under the Official Secrets Act he wrote several books from the early 1980s, donating the royalties to charity. Through these and the success of the James Bond 007 books and films, he gained a level of celebrity status when it came to light that the Bond author Ian Fleming (who had died in 1964) had probably based his SIS/MI6 Quartermaster character, 'Q', on Fraser-Smith. Fleming, while serving in Naval Intelligence, had worked with Fraser-Smith during the war and had appreciated the latter's aptitude for gadgets. One of Fraser-Smith's inventions, a compass hidden in a golf ball, was depicted in the 1971 James Bond film, '*Diamonds are Forever*'.

Ian Fleming, author of the James Bond novels, liaised with Fraser-Smith when Fleming was serving in Naval Intelligence. Photo: author's coll.

Fraser-Smith in later life with several of his gadgets. Photo: author's coll.

Fraser-Smith kept examples of most of his gadgets and once a year, would spend a week explaining their workings to visitors at Exmoor Steam Railway, a tourist attraction in Bratton Fleming in Devon that had an exhibit of his wartime works. He died at his home in 1992, survived by his second wife, Selina, and his two children, Brian and Christine, by his first marriage to Blanche who had died in1965. After his death, *Live and Let's Spy: an exhibition of spy, escape and survival gadgetry*, was created at Dover Castle by the then English Heritage (now Heritage England) and ran for two years in the late 1990s.

Sources and recommended further reading: '*The Secret War of Charles Fraser-Smith*' by Charles Fraser-Smith (Paternoster Press, 1981. ISBN 0-9528408-0-4 and '*The Man Who Was 'Q*', by David Porter (Paternoster Press, 1989. ISBN 0-85364-481-0.

CHAPTER 12

FLIGHT LIEUTENANT STEPHEN HANKEY 161 (SPECIAL DUTIES) SQUADRON, ROYAL AIR FORCE

Photo: author's coll.

BORN AT WESTHAMPNETT IN SUSSEX ON 17 AUGUST 1915, STEPHEN

Alers Hankey was the son of Colonel Cecil George Herbert Alers Hankey JP DL (a Deputy Lieutenant for Sussex), Royal Sussex Regiment, and Gertrude Clare Hankey (nee Fetherstonhaugh) of Binderton House, Chichester in Sussex. Stephen was the youngest of the family, having one sister and three brothers. While at Lancing College from September 1929 to 1934 he was a Corporal in the college's Officer Training Corps (OTC) and Captain of the Boxing Team. He gained his School Certificate in 1933 and in 1934, initially seeking to follow his father in an army career, Hankey went on to the Royal Military College, Sandhurst where he boxed for the college. During one of his bouts, he suffered a badly-broken nose which was to give him considerable pain when he later became a pilot. Upon leaving Sandhurst, he was commissioned as a 2nd Lieutenant in his father's regiment, the Royal Sussex Regiment, but resigned his commission in September 1937 in order to join the Delahaye company in London where he sold sports cars.

The Lancing College OTC's shooting team in 1933. Hankey is believed to be the Corporal on the extreme left of the row seated on chairs. Photo: Lancing College.

As war clouds gathered over Europe, he joined the Royal Air Force on a short service commission with the rank of Pilot Officer and service number 40822 on 4 June 1938 and on 26 July of the same year he was married at Chippenham to Elizabeth Anne Papillon of South Kensington, London, the daughter of one of his father's closest friends and a fellow-officer in the Royal Sussex Regiment during the Boer War. On the outbreak of war Stephen was serving with the RAF's 4 Squadron in an army co-operation role, flying Westland Lysander aircraft. He left for France with the squadron in September 1939, his wife went with him during this period and stayed in Paris. On 14 May 1940 he was flying a Lysander on a reconnaissance sortie when the aircraft crashed at the advanced landing ground at Aspelaere [now Aspelare] in Belgium. The aircraft was a write-off, but Hankey and his crewman, Sergeant Lewis, were both unhurt. During the Battle of France, 4 Squadron lost nearly all its aircraft, mostly to enemy action, and returned to England in late May 1940. Hankey was promoted to Flying Officer in September of that year and to Flight Lieutenant a year later, in September 1941.

After his return to Britain, Hankey was posted to the Middle East where he flew for a photographic reconnaissance squadron and then spent a period instructing Commonwealth trainee pilots. Thereafter he wore a tunic with each button being from a different air force to represent the various nationalities that he had trained. In June 1943 he returned to Britain with a posting to 161 (Special Duties) Squadron. The squadron flew in support of clandestine operations in occupied Europe and though the main base for its longer-range aircraft was at RAF Tempsford in Northamptonshire, 161 Squadron's A Flight operated the shorter-range Lysander aircraft from RAF Tangmere near Chichester in Sussex, close to where Hankey had been born. His wife moved with him, taking a cottage near Tangmere. Hankey spent much of June, July and August of 1943 in training, as although he was well-accustomed to flying the Lysander, he was not very experienced in night flying.

Hankey was a well-experienced pilot in the Lysander aircraft. Photo: author's coll.

In September 1943 he was cleared for operational flying and on the night of the 13/14 September he flew OPERATION DAISY to France for the Secret Intelligence Service (SIS/MI6) to collect an agent bringing Swiss mechanisms to England. Having picked up the man from near Dreux, Hankey was returning to base when he experienced complete electrical and radio failure while over Cabourg, but landed safely at RAF Tangmere. The following night he flew OPERATION GLADIOLA which involved flying to a farm near Baudreville to the north of Orléans. In the event he failed to pick up his passenger as there was no reception committee for him when he arrived over the field and he was forced to return to base. The next night he flew OPERATION DAMSON TREE, but again returned to base when he could spot no lights at the landing ground south-east of Chartres. On the night of the 18/19 September he flew OPERATION STOCKS for SIS/MI6 to a field north of Orléans, near Baigneaux, successfully delivering the agent Philip Keun and bringing out agent Félix Jonc and 18 parcels destined for the Ministry of Economic Warfare. The following month he flew OPERATION PILOT on 16/17 October to the BRONCHITE landing ground near Amboise where he landed agents Arthur Watt and Rémy Clément of French Section, SOE. On the return journey he brought back French Section SOE agent Maurice Southgate and two others. On the night of 9/10 November he took part in OPERATION ORIEL to the south-east of Châtellerault, but the operation had to be abandoned due to very bad weather. Similarly, he was 15 miles inside France on OPERATION GITANE on 16/17 November when he was forced to turn back because the cloud base was "down to the ground".

Hankey's final and fateful operation came on the night of 16/17 December 1943 when he was returning to Tangmere flying Lysander V9674, having successfully picked up two agents of the Free French intelligence service, the *Bureau Central de Renseignements et d'Action* (BCRA) to be brought to England from France in OPERATION DIABLE. Due to fog blanketing Tangmere, they diverted to the airfield at Ford, near Littlehampton in Sussex, but conditions were no better there and they crashed trying to land in the thick fog at 04:02. Hankey was killed instantly and the two French agents were mortally injured. Albert Kohan died that night and Jacques Tayar the following day. Both were buried in the Free French plot at the Brookwood Military Cemetery near Woking in Surrey. Tayar's headstone gives his true name and correctly describes him as a (former) naval officer, but Kohan is buried beneath a cross that lists him under his false identity of Lieutenant-Colonel Albert Berthaud.

Albert Kohan (a.k.a. Albert Berthaud) and Jacques Tayar (right) both died following the Lysander crash in bad weather. Photos: author's coll.

Kohan and Tayar are both buried in Brookwood Military Cemtery in Surrey, though Kohan's headstone erroneously shows his assumed identity. Photo: author.

The family's portrait of Stephen Hankey. Photo: Stephanie Griswold.

The grave of Hankey. Photo: author.

It had been a tragic night for 161 Squadron. Another Lysander also crashed while trying to land at Ford, killing the pilot, Flight Lieutenant James McBride, although his two passengers survived. And two Halifax aircraft, returning from France to the squadron's home base at Tempsford, also crashed, killing a total of four crew members. Squadron Leader Hugh Verity, a former 161 Squadron Lysander pilot, but then serving as SOE's Air Liaison – Operations officer, happened to be at Tangmere that night and later described the tragic events: "I had a bath, shaved, ate some breakfast, and telephoned Stephen's mother-in-law….I went down to see Stephen's wife. It was a harrowing business, but I felt I couldn't go home until it had been done." Hankey's wife, Elizabeth, was pregnant at the time and gave birth to twin daughters in May 1944.

Hankey was 28 years old when he was killed, he was buried in St George's Churchyard at Crowhurst in Sussex where his wife's family had a large estate. He is commemorated on the Crowhurst and Lancing College war memorials.

Sources and acknowledgements: Lesley Edwards, Archivist and Dr Mark Palmer at Lancing College; Stephanie Griswold and Roger P. Griswold.

PART 4

POST-WAR

CHAPTER 13

THE COST

TOWARDS THE END OF THE WAR IN EUROPE, LORD SELBORNE ARGUED
for retaining SOE, or a similar body, and in May 1945 he wrote:

> 'In view of the Russian menace, the situation in Italy, Central Europe and the
> Balkans and the smouldering volcanoes in the Middle East, I think it would be
> madness to allow SOE to be stifled at this juncture.'

Selborne's suggestion was that SOE ought to continue and should report to the
Ministry of Defence. But before a decision had been made, Prime Minister Churchill,
potentially the organisation's strongest supporter, lost the general election of July 1945.
His replacement, Clement Atlee, with strong lobbying from SIS/MI6, decided that SOE
had served its wartime purpose and should be closed down. It was officially dissolved on
15 January 1946, at which time it had records of some 40,000 people, of many nationalities, who had worked in and with it at home and overseas during the course of the Second
World War. There were many more locally-recruited helpers of SOE abroad, of whom
records were never kept in London.

The achievements and failures of SOE are debated to an increasing extent, thanks to
the continuing release of the organisation's archives and in particular the personal files of
agents. Several of its agents have been glamorised in books and films, some accurately and
some not. Treachery, betrayal and amateurism were all undeniably present throughout SOE's
relatively brief existence and several tragic blunders and disasters (especially in respect of
the successful radio transmission deceptions, *funkspielen,* operated by the German security

services) in some of the country sections have made it difficult to defend the organisation against its detractors. Colonel Maurice Buckmaster, commanding French Section, accepted that many of those involved had indeed been amateurs, but that was an unavoidable aspect at a time of world war and the human resources needed to wage it. On the credit side, General Eisenhower credited French Section alone with shortening the war by six months and described it as "the equivalent of 15 Divisions."

The cost in human terms is reflected in SOE's Roll of Honour of those who died in its service. It contains some 800 names, but for many hundreds more there is no memorial. Yet despite fears that only half the agents despatched would survive, reality showed a much better survival rate. Taking French Section as an example, 104 agents did not return, representing a quarter of some 417 sent to the field.

It is also undeniable that SOE's activities at the very least gave hope to those populations suffering under the yoke of enemy occupation and repression. It developed the 'spirit of resistance' among those peoples by helping them to assist in the liberation of their country and thereby regain a measure of their former national pride that had been so badly damaged by occupation. This 'spirit of resistance' lives on today in the motto of the Special Forces Club, founded post-war in London in 1945 on the initiative of the last head of SOE, Major-General Sir Colin Gubbins, KCMG, DSO, MC. A small group of former SOE staff founded the club in premises in Knightsbridge and in addition to being open to former SOE colleagues, it was decided that membership should also be available to those who had served in the Resistance organisations of the formerly occupied countries with which SOE had worked. Members were also welcomed from the wartime special forces, such as the SAS, and other organisations and services who had operated clandestinely in enemy-held territory. The Club continues to honour the memory of those who served in SOE.

THE SECRET WW2 LEARNING NETWORK

THE SECRET WW2 LEARNING NETWORK IS AN EDUCATIONAL CHARITY established with the aim of creating greater public awareness of the contributions and experiences of the men and women who during the Second World War took part in Allied special operations, intelligence gathering and resistance – particularly in Britain and France.

The charity has established a unique partner network of specialist historians, researchers, writers, teachers, veterans' descendants and associations, museums, local communities, and media outlets who work proactively with the charity's Trustees and volunteers to instigate learning initiatives and special commemorative events. Access to a unique archive of filmed personal testimony from more than a hundred British 'secret warriors' and French resisters provides a key resource, and the charity's innovative approach regularly brings recognition to these remarkable wartime exploits and also to the cross-channel links that were forged.

The ultimate aim of The Secret WW2 Learning Network is to ensure that the wartime contributions and sacrifices of the 'secret warriors' will become their lasting legacy in both countries by continuing to engage, inform and inspire people of all ages.

For more information please visit www.secret-ww2.net

The Secret WW2 Learning Network is a registered charity no. 1156796

All royalties from this book have kindly been donated to the charity by the author.